Comments on The Autimom Club:

"I laughed, commiserated, and felt there was finally someone who 'got it'. Great read! A must for every AutiMom!"

Laurie Kurluk, 56, Mesa Az
Fitness coach and AutiGrandma

"Jack's Mom captures the struggle felt by parents with children on the spectrum through hilarious anecdotes and grace! A true glimpse into the world and a must read for those wishing to understand what it's like to cope with autism in daily life."

Rose Rae, 25, Huntington Beach, CA
Teacher, AutiSister, Parent of Twins on the Spectrum

"I'm utterly blown away by this insightful book!"

Michael Oyler, 61, Arcadia, CA
Special Education Teacher

"I taught adaptive skiing to children on the spectrum and had a pretty good idea what life is like as an auti-parent? Wrong! *The Autimom Club* gives a thorough and hilarious tour of the auti-world. Mind-bending, heartbreaking, and delightful. A must read."

Mikaela Stanfield 32, Colorado Springs, CO
Bartender, Mother of Two

"I relished the delicious balance of help, hope and humor! One does not have to have an autistic member of the family to appreciate and enjoy this read."

"Karen Sandvic-Colasinski, 58, Ventura CA
Grandmother, Non-fiction Author

"This book welcomes you with the warmth of a girlfriend and a good cup of coffee."

Kari Kirby, 57, San Diego, CA
Recreational Therapist, Mother of Child with Autism

"The reader unraveling the mysteries of her own child's mind and looking for respite from dry medical advice will find this 'auti-mom' relatable and funny while providing anecdotes that inform and inspire."

"Diane Versaggi, 56, Big Bear Lake, CA
Mother of Two, Friend of Child with Autism

"An enjoyable read filled with relatable struggles and heartwarming triumphs felt by all individuals who have family members or close friends on the spectrum

Ramona Reiss, 69, Orange County CA
Computer Sales, Parent of Child with Asperger's

The AutiMom Club

Jack's Mom

Dedication

To my precious kids who, when after no parenting book proved useful for raising you, suffered under my loving but half-baked trial and error. Mostly error. You may send me your therapy bills. In the meantime, I couldn't be prouder of you!

Contents

Preface

I had my first child late in life, after travelling the world and starting my own company. My husband and I had decent financial padding at the time, along with great friends and a promising future. We felt ready for anything. And I'm guessing the cosmos took that as a challenge.

In his second year of life, our beautiful son, Jack, began slipping away. His pediatrician wouldn't pinpoint the problem for another 18 months. Meanwhile my husband and I began arguing regularly over what was or was not happening to Jack. The damage this did to our marriage and my business would be critical. More importantly, it delayed our son's access to that crucial early-interventive care that children with autism need. A sort of "mental calcification" set in that would leave Jack functionally-nonverbal until he was nine years old.

While balancing two jobs, giving birth to my second child — a daughter — shuttering my company, and surviving bankruptcy, I put together an intense therapeutic regimen for Jack to help break the grip autism had on him. I also read more books on the subject than I thought could even exist. For years I lived the life these books seemed to imply was necessary: Grim, joyless and determined. Yet almost daily, Jack did something brilliant or downright hilarious that would take my breath away. He was like a crazy, irrepressible flower springing up in the middle of a freeway. This beautiful side of autism wasn't mentioned in any of the books I'd read, and it's no exaggeration to say that Jack saved me, even as I was working to save him. I knew there were other AutiMoms out there who were wading through similar sorrows as mine, and who needed laughter and inspiration every bit as much as I did. So I began taking notes, determined to someday tell an autism story of cheer. Assuming I survived all the other stuff!

The AutiMom Club is the fruit borne of the years watching my son rediscover the world; all the bizarre, annoying, panicked, silly and magical moments that crowded our days. It's designed not to tell other AutiMoms what to do, but to be simply be their friend and help them enjoy the lives they've found themselves living. I hope it will both console and delight.

This book would not have been possible without the wonderful friends that stayed close by my side during those harder days: Cynthia Claire, Karlie Kohones, Amy Stokka, Kelly Izard, Diane M.B. Jones, Karen Colasinski, and Blake West — thank you for never giving up on Jack! I'm also deeply grateful to Wil Romero and Nikki Pfeiffer who gave Jack jaw-dropping opportunities to express himself; and Kelley Geddes, who was the first one (other than me!) who saw true brilliance in my son. More, and undying gratitude goes to my long-time friend Lawrence Riggins, who edited and shaped this book and basically dragged me over the finish line. I'd also like to thank my darling daughter, Annelise, who has spent her whole life patiently waiting for me while I worked with her older brother. And finally, let me thank Jack for teaching me to slow down, focus and appreciate what's directly in front of me. You have changed me completely.

"He who has a why can bear almost any how."

—*Frederich Nietzshe*

1

AutiMoms Unite!

I'm a fellow mom of a child with autism, and I know what you're going through. Between physical therapy, speech therapy, occupational therapy, feeding therapy and behavioral therapy, autism discussion group-monitoring, medical and homeopathic specialists, IEP meetings and meal planning (got one or more kids on a specialized diet? Woo-hoo! Bonus!), plus housework, homework, floor time, government forms and your personal extra — for me, sign language classes — . . . *it can be hard to get to work on time!* Ha-ha-ha, sigh.

This is Year Twelve for me, and I'll confess I've gone a little ditzy. I do stuff like put the phone down to look for a pencil and paper, then pick up a few toys and whatnot as I move from room to room. I might notice that Jack's bed isn't made, so I'll quickly do that. Ew, and the fish tank needs cleaning. At every turn there are dozens of undone tasks in my path, so I just keep powering forward. Eventually the caller realizes I've forgotten all about him.

And I tend to do two things at once while thinking about a third, a habit that is rarely productive. You know, I once found my wallet in the refrigerator? I stared at it for a few minutes before it clicked that maybe some fridge-worthy item of similar size had gone into my purse by mistake. Checking, I found a stick of butter. It had softened and skewered itself through the paper onto my hairbrush.

Today I started a load of laundry only to find one of last week's loads had never gone into the dryer. This happens to me *a lot*, so when the kid's bathroom ran out of fresh washcloths mid-week, I should have known why. There they were; a good 15 washcloths still in the washer, spun up along the drum wall. And what was this larger, dark lump, all ripe with mildew?

Oh.

"Sweetie! I found your Brownie uniform!"

I'm not disorganized, alright? I'm just… overloaded. If my life had a dashboard, there would be two or more warning lights flashing at any given time. I know you know what I'm talking about.

The home of an AutiMom is in a constant state of alert, because every moment our kids are awake, they are physically, emotionally, socially and psychologically stumbling along the edge of a cliff. Our job is to run behind them all day screaming "Look Out!" until our lungs are sore and our voices are gone. And that's probably a good thing. Because if we had our voices when that family member stopped by just long enough to wonder aloud, "When was the last time you had your carpets cleaned," we might have SAID something! Ha-ha, oh yeah. We might have shared a few words fiery enough to burn the salon-fresh hairdo right off their heads.

And…we don't want to do that. They're family, they love us and they are trying. But between you and me, they'll never get it. They can't. Even therapists, who deal with autism for a living, don't appreciate the load they add to our backs when they say things like, (and yes, someone actually said this to me,) "All you have to do is drag your kids around in a parachute for 10 minutes apiece before mealtime."

Blinking mutely. I'm sorry, what?

Returning our gaze. Is there a problem?

Because to them, see, ten minutes is a compact time unit that might otherwise be spent painting toenails or reading Facebook posts. Trading this seemingly useless time unit to pull a child (or two) around in a parachute is absolutely reasonable. It's simply a matter of priorities!

But *you've already* given up every useless unit of time in your possession. Your Facebook profile is so out of date that it's yellowing around the edges. Your utterly un-pampered toenails have devolved into claws. And honestly, when was the last time you relaxed with a glass of wine, or watched an entire show, or even soaked in the bathtub? I wear a track suit to bed so I can wake up and hit the ground running. My day is streamlined, air-tight, freeze-dried and shrink-wrapped. Those ten minutes of parachute-dragging before every meal can only be extracted from what remains of my meager ration of sleep. So, yes! *Yes, there is a problem!* And by the way, where is the study supporting the claim that 10 minutes in a parachute for each of my two kids, three times a day will show results sufficient to compensate for my giving up 60 more minutes of sleep every night, 7 nights a week, month after month, for the foreseeable future? And that's after I spend another precious hour (and maybe 50 bucks) acquiring the necessary parachute, because let's be honest, if I'd had a parachute to begin with, *I would have jumped already!*

Flash Rant Alert!

Right. I'm only 800 words into this thing and I've already written myself into a frenzy. My brain says, "Go back and delete it." My heart says, "Make me, you fat grey blob!" I'm with Heart: You have a right to know that you're not the only one going insta-berserk. Sometimes, when you have a barking Flash Rant straining the leash, the best thing to do is let it loose. Let the rant purge you of all negative energy, and re-center you in lavender-scented serene Zen-iness. Check it out: I feel better already!

Now, where was I?

The great thing about autism is the kids it produces. I think my children are downright magical, and I enjoy my time with them more every day. I finally know what I'm doing. I've figured out what they need from me and how to push them forward a bit every day while keeping life in a reasonable balance. They are thriving, and they're at that point where I'm secretly starting to suspect they're superior to other kids. (Shh! Don't tell people I said that or they'll stop bringing me casseroles!)

Sure, I expect to be time-starved for another few years. Yes, I could use more money. I also wouldn't turn down a new wardrobe, a full-time assistant and maybe one of those massage chairs. But life on the whole is sweet. So whatever you're going through right now on your own journey with autism, trust me when I tell you it's going to be worth it.

The Margarita Dilemma

The one thing I'm really craving, though, is the chance to sit down with other moms and engage in the classic trifecta of Girls Night Out: Bitching, laughing and drinking margaritas. I really miss the comradery I used to have with my other mom-friends. I've tried to maintain that connection, and my friends, bless their hearts, have been really good sports about it. But as you've probably already discovered on your own, it's hard to swap tales with friends who have neurotypical kids.

"My eight-year-old will be playing Clara in the Youth Ballet's Nutcracker this year!"

Yay! Can you get us tickets?

"My five-year-old was accepted into the Buddy Werner Ski Racing League! His first race is next weekend!"

Awesome! Next stop, the Olympics!

"I'm proud to announce that my six year old has learned to use the potty all by himself!"

(Frozen half-smiles.)

Come on, people! My news is more life-critical, and the tale that

5

goes with this potty-training news is ingenious (if I do say so myself). But nonAutiMoms are stopped cold by our stories as they calculate the socially proper response. Should they laugh, and if so, are they laughing in the right places? Does a loud laugh prove that they're laughing *with* us and not *at* us? Or does a soft chuckle say that better? They might glance at each other for help, or nervously close your topic down with a shake of the head and a sad, "I don't know how you do it."

Watching our friends grapple with Response Anxiety can be painful. I've thought about bringing one of those mood charts the therapists use: "Okay ladies, I'm moving the magnet frame over to bi-i-ig happy face. See? That means you can *laugh* now!"

And what about bitching? Our friends are supposed to gasp and growl and slap the table with, "Damn right, sister!" That's the way it works in the official Girlfriend's Code of Conduct: You've got the *bitch-or*, who is the one monologing for a reasonable stretch of time, and the *bitch-ees*, who gasp and growl and hog the guacamole, and who jab chips at the air in regular intervals saying, "Damn right, sister!" But now our friends seem unsure that this classic response is appropriate. They may have decided that their own gripes are petty, leaving them feeling guilty or uncomfortable venting as they used to. The drama-log and Greek chorus of Girls Night bitching have become calm, civilized exchanges separated by periods of quiet chip-munching.

It goes without saying that our friends are doing nothing wrong. But the success of a friendship hinges on the things that we have in common. Let's face it: A central chunk of our lives no longer has anything in common with the lives of our friends. We're now foreigners in our own social circle. After a while, even our best friends start getting together without us. And you know it's true, so go on and admit it: *You're glad to be rid of the pressure.*

But that leaves us alone with our stories; stories that deserve an audience equipped to meet them head-on without discomfort. Our stories are rich and funny and shocking, sometimes heartbreaking or infuriating, but always huge! How many times have you seen your child struggle to learn something — with horrid, clumsy, gawdawfulness — for month upon month, until you gave up and crossed that activity off some mental list of things he might someday do. Then, long after you've forgotten about it, he suddenly has it *mastered*, leaving you to wonder how?! The more I dissect Jack's everyday accomplishments, the more I'm struck by the isolation, resolve and downright heroism of my boy.

So YES, my friend. We must stand up for ours stories! Stories of hope, valor and what-the-hell-just-happened?! These are the most worthwhile stories to be heard at any Girl's Night get-together, but also the least likely to be told... *until now*! So let the

AutiMom Pact be forged! For the next however-many-pages-this-turns-out-to-be, we will bitch, laugh and drink margaritas. Let us start by toasting to our fabulous kids!

2

What Day Is It Anyway?

Do you ever find yourself wondering? Not just first thing in the morning after getting only 90 minutes of sleep, when you're brain-lagged by a decade or more, don't recognize your own bedroom and have no clue why that clock is beep-shrieking at you. *How do I turn this thing off?!*

Please. That's amateur hour.

I'm talking about the 2:00pm phone call from school about Thursday's IEP meeting, and maybe it's one you're actually prepared for: The folder is right there on the counter, completely organized, and it's only Wednesday. Boom! You're awesome! You even received a narrative summary back from the pediatrician, which makes you the super-on-top-of-it Best-Mom-The-School-Has-Ever-Seen! But the woman on the phone sounds miffed and cuts you off in the middle of your bragging. She needs to reschedule because you didn't show up at the meeting. Today's not Wednesday, it's Friday.

Wait, what?!

And now you don't hear anything else she says because your mind is busy telescoping out, revealing two days-worth of stuff you missed: A dental appointment, gymnastics class, behavioral therapy, a Scout meeting… Really?! Not ONE person called to complain about your absence?!

Surprise: You have 13 messages from 20 missed calls. You really need to check more often. And by the way, a Post-it on your shopping list is screaming, "Scout Snacks!!!" because it was your week to feed them. You pull the note, crumple it, and balance it on top of the kitchen trash, which is overflowing, and oh yeah you missed the garbage truck today.

Insert curse word here, my friend.

That's what I'm talking about! Being as wide awake as you're ever gonna get, and still not knowing what day it is!

It's not your fault. When you're living the AutiMom life, you are rushed, stressed, pressured and exhausted every minute of every day.

And while all that has you distracted, the playful Gods of Quantum Displacement are busy scrambling your calendar. Days disappear and get reinserted at random. Oh, you thought it was just your imagination? It's real, sister. Yet somehow society expects us to adhere to the static and organized linear calendar that everyone else enjoys. Pffft. Good luck with that.

I don't know. Maybe we should blame society for holding our households to some arbitrary, neuro-normative standard? (Awesome! I just made that phrase up, and it sounds totally social-sciencey!) I'm tired of apologizing for missing stuff, or arriving a day early, or showing up at the wrong venue when everybody else somehow magically knew that we were meeting across town this time! I could use some little cards to hand out at moments like this:

"Personal Policy Statement: I only say, "Sorry," after punching someone in the face, so... how badly do you want that apology?"

Margarita Moment:

Ever woke up on a school day thinking it was Saturday? Face-palm extreme. You get to sheepishly drop those kids off at school several hours late. But! When your kids are nonverbal, you're free to tell the

school any old fib on the fly without
fearing they will rat you out! Cheers!

Dates, times, the speed limit, the amount of money still in my
checking account, how many kids I left the house with... Anything
to do with numbers will zip right out of my brain when I'm under
stress, which is pretty much always. So I don't know where Jack
gets it: Jack's relationship with numbers is mindboggling. He
doesn't think about them in terms of a typical number line, with 0
on one end and infinity somewhere out there on the other, but as a
3 dimensional grid – like a gigantic parking structure, where every
number's possible relation to every other number in the structure
has an assigned space. I'm starting to think he's not really my child!

Diary Note: Today is April 5th. When I
woke Jack up this morning, he
announced he'd been twelve years old
for 198 days, that it was his 134th day
of 6th grade, and that Easter was 1,827
minutes away (mountain day-light
savings time, for those of you needing
more accuracy). He didn't even have to
think about it.

Jack loves all things based on numbers. Clocks, calculators, calendars… Each New Year's, he hangs 15 calendars in his room before running out of good locations. The stack of leftovers on his desk right now is almost eight inches high. There are more in his closet from previous years, which I am not allowed to throw out. At one point, I sneaked one of those plastic tubs into his closet to corral them, but the calendars crested the rim in 2017. Now they rise in a precarious tower, ready to slither apart and cascade to the floor at the slightest disturbance. Retrieving his laundry basket each week is a mission worthy of Special Ops.

Jack has every one of those calendars memorized down to the phases of the moon. Some of them have Canadian, European or Asian holidays on them. Some are in foreign languages. All this data has been uploaded and stored in the mathematical grid in his head. You want to treat your family to a cruise on the Indian Riviera during Ram Navami (which, as you know, occurs on day nine of the Hindu Lunar New Year)? Jack can tell you when to book it.

No one ever taught him how to calculate this kind of thing. So how would he know, for example, what day-of-the-week a date will fall on in some future year; that you need to take 365 x 3 + 366, then divide that by 4, then multiply it by the difference of the year you want and the year you're currently in, then divide that by 52 and add the results to the day of the week that the date in question fell on this year… so I guess you'd have to know that for starters wouldn't you? Beats me, Girlfriend, I'm making this up. I don't know how the heck you would calculate it!

And anyway, Jack doesn't bother with calculations. He has an assigned parking space in his brain where the answer already sits. All he has to do is reach in and grab it.

The first time he did this for me, he was 4 years old and still 5 years away from functional speech. I talked out loud all the time back then to sort of "baste" Jack with the rhythms and melody of language, and I guess I was blabbering on about his dad's birthday, which was still several months off. I wasn't aware I'd posed a question when I heard Jack pipe up, "Friday."

"Do you need something, sweetie?"

"No! Friday! Friday!" He waved me away with this little wrist move he had for shooing off irritants of all types.

Obediently, I withdrew from his room.

I didn't plan to check the computer calendar downstairs to see if "Friday" and "Dad's birthday" overlapped, but there I was anyway. Interestingly, they did indeed overlap. I thought, "Huh. Fun coincidence."

(Really? That's the end of it?)

There was a juice cup on the desk, so I picked it up and took it into the kitchen to place it into the dishwasher. But I never got that far. Instead, I found myself creeping back up the stairs to Jack's door, juice cup still in hand. "Jack," I asked softly.

"No!" Wrist-wave, wrist-wave.

"What day is Dad's birthday on in 2025?"

Shouting angrily, "Tuesday! Tuesday!" *Go away, Mom! Stop asking lame questions!*

And he was right. Seeing it confirmed on the computer calendar left me dazed and proud, but sort of freaked out — as if the parakeet had gotten out of its cage and started working on my tax return. It was *U N R E A L*, and in that instant, everything changed! Should I call Jack's doctor? Should I call the school? Should I call the news station? And by the way, how was I supposed to raise someone who is *that much smarter than I am?*

This last question has yet to be answered. I'll keep you posted. In the meantime, I'm doing the best I can! But if you happen to catch me sitting stupefied somewhere while my children are nearby setting fires or drinking bleach, give me a good slap in the face, would you?

Margarita Moment:

(Two margaritas in one chapter? Awesome!)

Family lore long held that my mother was born on Friday the 13th, was married on Friday the 13th and gave birth to her first child on Friday the 13th. She firmly believed in the good-luck power of 13 and assured us that any event tied to a Friday the 13th received the kiss of greatness. A few weeks ago, I was passing this family treasure on to my daughter as Jack happened to enter the kitchen. "Grandma Betsy was born on Sunday," he said. Then he opened his Coke and left the room.

3

Grovelingly Loyal

AutiMotherhood comes with some true bennies. One is "waking up" to the kindness already present in the people, schools, and businesses that you already know. Once you see it, you wonder how you managed to miss it all that time!

Of course, not everyone is kind. The world has produced a bumper-crop of A-holes, but you don't need to put up with them. Allow me, in fact, to insist that you don't. The energy you waste in everyday A-hole-defense is needed for a higher purpose now. Discover and cling to the people who show your child kindness. Before you know it, you will be living in a protective snow globe of loveliness.

Jack was seven and we were in the toy section of Target. His intense study of the Thomas The Tank Engine train collection was suddenly interrupted by him wetting his pants. And wow. A seven year old kid carries a lot of liquid: The puddle went three feet out in every direction!

Angry and disoriented, Jack began shouting.

Job one? Prevent "environmental escalation."

You know what I mean: A gathering crowd of gawkers, someone pointing or yelling at him, Jack slipping in urine, the usual stuff. I needed to extract him from the scene and corral him where I'd have better control of his surroundings. I took his hand and walked him to the family bathroom in the front of the store, flagging a staff member en route with a fast-whispered, "Clean up on the Thomas aisle!"

Once in the bathroom, Jack began stripping down, which hadn't been my plan! Actually, I hadn't really *had* a plan beyond fleeing the scene, but skipping out of the store with a naked child did not meet my minimum standards for good planning, low as those standards had become. But you know how it is: Once our kiddos get a head of steam going, it can be truly difficult to change directions without causing a screaming meltdown. So this was pretty much going to be what I had to work with. Naked child.

Wait a minute... I was at Target! I could just *buy* him *dry clothes*! That would be much easier than forcing Jack back into his cold, soggy pants. At least he still had his shirt on. This would work! So I told my functionally non-verbal seven year-old to wait in this small, windowless room while I shopped for clothes. You can see where this is going.

I moved fast, of course; undies, pants, socks, shoes, grabbing the first of each that I saw in his size. I would buy them as we left the store, so I was on my way back to the bathroom in under four minutes. It was still too long.

Sprinting down the main aisle, I heard a walkie talkie go off: "Uh… I've got a complaint about a half-naked boy in Toys…"

Right? These things don't even sound weird to us anymore.

"That's my son!"

I switched directions, linked the employee by the elbow and dragged her along with me toward the toy department. Bless her heart, she didn't flinch. As I shared my tale with her, she snapped up her walkie talkie and called all available staff members. They emerged from everywhere like magic and joined us on our mighty quest to re-pant my child.

On the Thomas Aisle, two "Wet Floor" signs marked the scene of our previous crime. Between them now stood Jack, squealing and laughing, examining a lighted display case; free as a spirit from the waist down. My Target staff hostage stationed her team members at either end of the aisle to keep shoppers away and to give Jack some privacy. Then it was up to me. Like an entrant in a timed calf-roping contest, I ripped the tags off the new clothing and dressed Jack where he stood. "Finished!"

The emergency was over, Jack went back to studying the trains, and eight Target employees were now looking at me. They didn't shift their feet or try to slink off without making eye contact; they did something quite natural: They started laughing. It was a laugh of relief and kindness, as if this could have happened to any one of them. My former hostage asked if I was okay and if I needed anything else, then she wished us a good evening and everyone went back to work. I've been utterly loyal to this store ever since.

Awesome work, Target! This is how it's done![1]

---

[1] In 2016, I nominated Target for an Arc Award for Outstanding Customer Service to the Disabled Community. I'm pleased to tell you they won.

Weird Autism Myth #1

Autism is a Result of Poor Parenting

The sound coming from my lips right now has no name, but it's halfway between a sigh and a snarl (a snigh?) I'm telling you. Google this lazy and outright insulting phrase and you'll be ogling reams of studies and stories that have been written on the topic. Go ahead: Google and ogle. I'll wait.

It's enough to make your head explode, isn't it? When do AutiParents get to counter with their own research on how "Autism Myths are a Result of Poor Social Science Practices"? That might shock the monocles out of a few snooty eye sockets!

(I'm pretty sure social scientists don't wear monocles anymore. I should update my snark.)

While I agree "Not All Mothers Are Created Equal," I'd like to propose a radical new theory: *AutiMoms* are the *better* moms because our kids forge us into it. We *become* better mothers because our everyday lives *demand* it of us (and the alternative is to be hauled off in a straitjacket while our homes burn to the ground.) Yes, our kids are charming, noble and fascinating, but they're also wild, inscrutable, infuriating and sometimes dangerous. They give us daily Nautilus-style motherhood weight-training workouts which leave us strong and ready to take on challenges that lesser mothers would flee from weeping with fright!

For proof, let me share this simple, personal story from the World of Neurotypicals:

Did I mention this story was about me? Yeah, it is. Sorry. I talk about myself a lot.

Sigh, tap-tap-tap....

I blame it on this medium, okay? It prevents *you* from talking to *me*. However, if this book has a point – and I'm not sure it does, but let's say for the sake of argument that it does – that point would be to assure you that I hear you anyway! We *all* hear you. You have the loudest voice at the table and we will not let you be silenced! Got that? Are we good?

Have some chips.

Okay. Back to me:

I was the fourth child born in quick succession to a mother who still worked as a model in Los Angeles. Think about how exhausted and undernourished this must have left her! Right? So, when I was three weeks old, she took me on a call-back for a lipstick commercial. I'm pretty sure I helped her get the job – who can resist a big-eyed newborn in a car seat carrier? But when she went back to her car, she put the carrier on the roof while she opened the door and stowed her purse and portfolio. Then she got in the car, started the motor and pulled away from the curb. True story.

So there I was, roof-surfing down Santa Monica Boulevard in rush-hour traffic. Mom ignored the honking and yelling from neighboring drivers, as beautiful women tend to do. *Yes, boys, eat your hearts out.* Eventually, one kind man edged his vehicle into my mom's and pushed her off the road. He saved my life. Thank you Kind Man, wherever you are!

May this tale of Jack's Mom's Mom help you recover from the shame of whatever Mom-Crime you may think you've committed today! I'm sorry, what? You ran out of baby carrots and had to put cucumber slices in your child's lunch today? What kind of a monster are you?!

Now. Are you ready for the psychological twist?

My mom didn't bother telling me this story until after my son was born. And it wasn't, "Now that you're a mom we can have mom-to-mom talks," it was more, "Now that you're a mom, my job is done. I'm post-mom and no longer responsible for the idiotic things I did as a mom." She laughed herself into a coughing fit as she recounted this long-ago moment of ditzy glamour, while I sat with a jaw so slackened that I burned my chin in my coffee. She was dusting her hands of maternal duty and letting me know I should not come to her for advice. She may have also been warding off any future babysitting requests.

Gotta tell you, girlfriend, it worked: I love my mom to bits, but I've never once left my kids with her.

So, no. Not all moms are created equal, even when they share the same DNA. You might want to remind yourself of this the next you enter one of those critic-infested social gatherings that crouch on your calendar near any holiday.

Attention AutiMoms:

If you're expecting visitors – particularly meddling, know-it-all types – I recommend you place a book mark in the next page and leave this book lying in some conspicuous location. Your meddling visitors are bound to snoop. Hopefully they'll learn something. Cheers!

Alarming Causes of Autism!*

Please check all relevant boxes:

☐ During pregnancy, were you ever within 100 feet of someone using a cell phone?

☐ Does your child play with any toys that were made in China?

☐ Do you, or have you ever, use(d) the microwave oven whild your child is in the room (including in utero)?

☐ Has your child been immunized?

☐ Has your child ever had a cold or fever?

☐ Does your child ever view any video displays, such as TVs, laptops, tablets or cell phones?

☐ If your child has siblings, were they born less than two years apart from your child?

☐ If your child has siblings, were they born more than four years apart from your child?

☐ Have you, or any member of your family, ever travelled outside of the continental United States?

☐ Have you or your child ever worn a disposable diaper?

☐ Have you, or any member of your family, ever put jam on your toast without first applying butter?

☐ Does anyone close to you have two middle names?

☐ Do you ever continue reading survey questions even after deciding the survey is bogus?

If you have two or more boxes checked, your child may have autism. Contact our offices at once for thoroughly pricey diagnostics and an even pricier long-term intervention plan.

According to popular fads plus additional nonsense added by author.

4

Mom Has Notes

I suppose I've been mildly neurotic all my life, but having kids encouraged me to stop hiding it. Life in the AutiMom lane has now shifted my neurosis into overdrive.

As I'm sure you've noticed, the autism community is full of panic peddlers. Everyone's got an opinion to push, and the latest opinion is often in conflict with the opinion you just heard last week. There's always some new drug or vitamin or gadget or therapy or diet or homeopathic regimen that friends, relatives, support groups, acquaintances, what's-your-name-agains, or complete and utter strangers feel compelled to press on us: So-and-so swears by it! Her child was *cured in six weeks!*

Right… Is it just me? Or does it sometimes feel like a cult?

Most of the proclaimed causes and "cures" are as crazy as the pace with which new ones replace them. Each successive "program" spawns its own following, causing AutiMoms to be pummeled anew with propaganda from the freshly-informed busybodies in our orbit. Pitches are often paired with the threat that your "window of intervention is closing." Thank you for not punching these people — I know how badly you want to.

Nothing is more important to us than our children. That's what makes us such juicy targets for both the hype and the hype-serving products that spring up like weeds right behind it. If we don't guard ourselves with skepticism, we will spend all our time, money and energy chasing shadows. Worse, we will spend all our hope.

The Scoop on Hope

It's a finite resource. Once hope is gone, human beings slow to a stop. We hunker down and live life in the smallest way possible, sort of waiting for things to end. Feeling like this at thirty is bad enough. But if you're three, and the people responsible for your wellbeing have fallen into the dire funk of hopelessness, you're in serious trouble.

Okay, let's cut people some slack. Those folks shoving the latest fads in our faces are *trying* to help. They think they're giving us "new hope". But hope isn't an external resource. It can't be given; it can only be spent. So say, "Thank you," then drop the pamphlet in a drawer. If the regimen is right for your child, that pamphlet will call out to you in the wee hours of the morning. But odds are it won't. Ground yourself, and spend your hope with miserly restraint.

Now, Back to My Neuroses!

They told me my son has autism, but they couldn't tell me what that meant. He might speak some day or he might not. Maybe he'll sleep so deeply I'll think he's dead, or maybe he'll barely sleep at all. He might eat well, or way too much, or starve himself right into the hospital, or maybe he'll eat rocks and cat poop. And he could turn out to be a Nobel Prize-winning math wizard! Then again, he might sit in a corner rocking himself while repeatedly counting to 100. Who knows? That'll be $1,600, please. Sorry, we don't take insurance.

I'M HARDLY EVEN EXAGGERATING!!

They stamp "Autism" on your kid's forehead, hand you brochures for their pricey partner firms specializing in diet and therapies, and call "Next!" What more can they do in 15 minutes — our kids are all too different! At some point I stopped even asking for guidance. I began looking at Jack as if he were a boy with a unique medical condition, and assumed most insights about him would go from me to the Med Pros, not the other way around.

Ball point clicking, I followed Jack around like some creepy vulture/stenographer. I had logs in almost every room of the house, noting Jack's daily intake and outgo, his activities, fixations, outbursts, sleep patterns, weight, height, gait, ailments, medicines, therapies, and daily skin "rating." I also had a separate log to keep track of my logs.

27

A few days before each doctor's appointment, I would compile my data and look for patterns that may have escaped me. I would then fax a list of recent observations to the doctor's office, and write up a separate list of questions that I would tuck into my purse for the day of the appointment.

They called me "obsessed,"
so I buried them in my data!

Once, while waiting for Jack's doctor to return to the examination room, I flipped open the file that he'd left on the counter. It was a fat, multi-divided monster, with a separate section just for my faxes. What struck me, though, were the words he had written on the inside cover of the file in thick marker:

"Mom Has Notes."

Why would he write that? Was he warning his staff that I was a law suit waiting to happen? Was he encouraging them to have confidence in the fidelity of my input? Or was he just flagging me as a psycho-mom? I never had the courage to ask. But at that moment, I realized my neurosis had turned me into a Seinfeld character. [2]

I didn't go full-on "Elaine Benes" and change doctors. But within six months of my snooping, Jack's doctor ditched the file folders for an electronic system. To date, I have not been left alone with the laptop. Who knows what Jack's file says about me by now...

Thumbs Up!

The suspected causes of autism, and methods for addressing it, continue to evolve. Every few years, a specialist wants to take a fresh look at Jack's history to consider his case from a different angle. No problem! All 12 years' worth of my logs on Jack sit in a file cabinet right here in my office, and believe me, they are a goldmine. There's no question too crazy or far back in time that I can't answer with accuracy. Kapow!

But the logs' greatest use has come when no doctor was around. Instead, based on some hunch or other, I reviewed half a year's-

---

[2] In case you haven't seen the episode, a horrified Elaine discovers notes that her doctor has been making about her. She tries to get rid of them, but the doctor finds out and writes even more notes about the deception. Panicked, Elaine changes doctors, but the damning notes from the previous doctor follow her into the new doctor's file. https://en.wikipedia.org/wiki/The_Package_(Seinfeld)

worth of data and discovered long, rolling patterns, or an intense cluster of events that subsided for no apparent reason, only to come back again months later. When your child is unable to tell you how he feels, this data is better than having a 24/7 personal psychic.

5

The $62 Discount

AutiMoms typically adore their Avon ladies. If you don't have one,
I might recommend finding one, even though my own experience
with the service was mixed. Here's the thing: Every minute an
AutiMom spends in a store is a minute spent poking fate in the eye.
When fate strikes back, things get ugly. Right? We *all* have horror
stories. Who needs more of *that* when Avon will send the store to
your home? Your Avon lady will also supply you with catalogs to
browse while you're sitting on the pot – a multitasking opportunity
that's generally discouraged at Walmart.

And there's the fun of having someone other than a therapist
come to your door. I'd invite my Avon lady in for a cup of coffee
while I wrote her a check, and I'd tell her a quick Jack story. She
always asked about Jack and seemed to enjoy hearing about him,
although she'd never met him; whenever she stopped by, he'd hide.
Sound familiar?

It probably does, and here's why I think that is: The parade of
new, in-home therapists our kiddos face goes on and on without

31

end. At the youngest ages, our kids figure out that those "people visiting Mom" are not really "visitors" and they're not there to "see Mom." They're can feel the Visitor's attention shifting away from Mom and reaching out with psychic fingers to explore the house, searching for the Child. Nonverbal kids are mega-alert to this kind of "threat," so they go radio-silent and hunker down behind the bed or in the closet, suppressing the urge to seek safety in Mom's lap while the Visitor is with her. If the Child even peeks around the corner, he might make eye contact with the Visitor. Then the Visitor will pounce! She'll spring from her chair to grab the fleeing Child by the leg, and drag him away to labor.

"Nooooooooooooooooooooooo!"

What.

Too over the top?

Fine. I realize these sessions are fun and our kids end up enjoying them, but you gotta admit, there's something primal in that early interaction. Why else would our kids hide?

Anyway, back to my story. Jack was nearing four at the time. He had a baby sister. He had learned to say "Maymay" (baby), "Fen" (friend), "Muttle" (bottle), and "Huk" (hug). And perhaps because he *did* have this sister now, and people were coming to coo and fuss over *her*, he found visitors less threatening. They were kind of interesting, even!

So today he heard Mom downstairs talking to a visitor and perhaps he heard his name being mentioned. Today he decided to meet this visitor and show her he had learned a fifth word.

The Avon lady and I were looking at a photo hanging on the wall near the foot of the stairs. Jack came halfway down the first flight of stairs, then leaped to the landing and crouched down in frog-like fashion. In a bold, happy voice, he said, "Frog!!" At least, that's what he was trying to say, and since I *knew* that's what he was trying to say, that's what I heard. But if you cross-reference "frog" with some of the other words Jack had mastered, mentioned above, you'll get a sense of what he actually said.

"Frog! Frog!" Jack bounced in his crouch.

"Yay! That's very good, Jack," I bubbled, as the Avon lady's coffee tickled onto the carpet. "What a nice boy for coming down to say hello!"

"Frog!"

I met Jack on the stairs and lifted him into my arms. He was getting so big, I wouldn't be able to do this much longer. When I turned to start back down the steps, the Avon lady was already buttoning her coat.

"I really shouldn't take up any more of your time," she said. "I'll see myself out."

"Wait, wouldn't you like to meet Jack?"

"Maybe next time!" She scrambled forth without glancing at us. "Bye you two!" The door opened and closed, and she was gone.

She had left the moisturizers on the kitchen counter. Beside them was the check I'd just written her for $62.

A good half-hour had passed before I realized what she thought she had heard Jack say. I laughed, mildly mortified over how it had unnerved her, and I planned to call her later to explain.

By dinnertime, though, the incident had gotten under my skin. She couldn't have been that upset without first making some kind of

33

weird, ugly assumption about my family. *She* owed *me* an apology! Until she called to make one, I gave myself permission to hold onto the check.

She never called or contacted me again.

So I don't have an Avon lady anymore. As for the inadvertent discount: I'm only sorry this last order hadn't been bigger!

Language Is Good!

All parents snap at their kids from time to time, and life in an AutiMom's home can be more stressful than others. It's not my intent to make you feel guilty for having ever snapped at your spectrum child. But if you need to scream, you might try screaming at someone who can understand and accept your apology afterwards. (Like that nice neighbor threatening to call the police.)

Our kiddos tend to avoid language and social encounters. The skills these require exhaust them, so they hold off until an emergency arises; they're hungry, cold, or their sister is hogging the video game console. I can't encourage you enough to make your verbal interactions with your spectrum child as rewarding to them as possible. Humor has always worked well for Jack, but I've also used games, snacks, pets, poopy sound-effects, or whatever it takes. The more our kids find enjoyment in the company of others, the quicker and more readily they will relate to the world outside their own heads.

6

Sherlock of Quirk

So... your nonverbal, diaper-wearing preschooler has never related to a peer. The paras drag him around the classroom like a sack of laundry. He gets stared and frowned at everywhere you go – or worse: I've actually seen alarmed mothers gather their children and flee, as if Jack were contagious. *Hey lady, you dropped your diaper bag... never mind. Ooo, cookies!*

Then suddenly, he proves he's smart. Not just smart, but smarter than *you*. Maybe the smartest person you've ever known. Now what? Yeah, go ahead and drop a voicemail on that snooty cousin who didn't invite you to her wedding because she didn't want your child wrecking her big day. "Whaddaya know! My kid has more wattage than that dork-with-a-man-bun you married! Ha-ha! Ha-ha-ha-ha-ha-ha-ha-ha!" (End.) Yeah, she deserves it. But then it's time to get serious. Where do you start?

That's a stumper. It doesn't help that our kiddos have a unique talent for making us feel inferior. Jack and I both now knew that I had little worth to him except as valet for his snacks and sunscreen. I shuffled along behind him for months like an indentured servant. *More juice, m'lord? Would you care for some animal crackers?*

Out of pity for what little dignity I still possessed, I began carrying a spiral notebook. My ability to write proved that I was superior to my four year old, so I adopted an air of importance by jotting notes as Jack fed ducks, tossed stones and flapped at passing poodles. I noted his squeals and squawks, his periods of quiet contemplation, and any attempt he might make at doing something new – climbing the ladder on a play structure, for example. As a rule, these attempts were quickly ditched, even when I offered to help him.

Hey! Did I just detect a pattern? How clever of me!

And here was another: He liked to watch other kids play. He'd laugh and flap and have such a great time about it that the kids invariably liked him. But as soon as they spoke to him, he'd squawk and run away.

And another: He liked to walk around parked cars, studying them from every angle.

And another: Jack would carry one green item in one hand and one matching red item in the other hand: Balls, blocks, markers, Dixie cups, whatever he happened upon, as long as there was a red and a green one available. He'd walked around with them and occasionally stop to bring them together at eye level.

And another: He'd run squealing toward the curb when he heard the ice cream man coming. But when the vehicle stopped for him, he'd wail at the driver hard enough to blow the speaker right off the top of the truck.

Your kid's doing this stuff too, right? No? Something else maybe? Okay, cool.

No, it *wasn't* cool at *all*. *Why was Jack doing these things?!*

We know how kids are: they all have odd routines. I used to wiggle my feet when I was concentrating. My daughter prefers to eat in bed with her head under the blankets. But Jack. Jack was a quirk-a-minute! And I couldn't pretend I didn't see them anymore because I had chosen to marry my pride to a notebook. These quirks now towered up from every page, wobbling, tipping over, smacking me in the face with the iron locks of their mystery. Damn right it was painful – almost as painful as reading that last sentence!

I noted the quirks as fast as I could spot them, and later would scour the pages for some kind of pattern. I flew through these notebooks. I also shot a lot cell phone video, hoping to catch Jack anytime he spoke – which, of course, wasn't often, since he technically wouldn't speak for another five years. But that suggested to me that when he *did* say something, there was a driving reason for it, and it was up to me to figure out what it was. I had a total Sherlock routine going as I circled my son to study, document and film him.

Did I mention mothers fled with their kids at the sight of my son? Ha-ha-ha, could be they fled at the sight of *me*!

But! I am proud to say that I did solve a few of these mysteries. Here is one of them:

THE ICE CREAM MAN COMETH

The sound of Yankee Doodle toning flatly from the roof-top speakers of the ice cream truck absolutely electrified my 4 year old son. He'd ditch his toy, jump to his feet and start running toward the music. There was something from that truck that he badly wanted, and over the course of the summer not once did I manage to choose it. Jack would scream and pace as I quickly surveyed the menu, picking bomb after bomb in a three-month exercise of frozen trial and error. I tried a Rainbow Pop. I tried a Strawberry Shortcake. I tried a ChacoTaco, a Creamsicle and a Fudge Bar. I tried an ice cream sandwich and a Push-up. Each time, the offered treat was swatted into the gutter with fury. I must have gone through $50 worth of ice cream that summer before giving up.

"I give up," I finally said, while signing emphatically, "I! Give! Up!"

The next time the ice cream truck entered the neighborhood, I stood there with my arms defiantly crossed. That'll teach him!

The ice cream man or Jack?

Didn't matter. They were both to blame.

The truck turned onto our street and its Yankee Doodle tones were instantly brighter. Jack watched it approach. His squeal-and-flap routine went Mach One until I thought he would lift off! How could I stay mad at this kid?

Laughing, I took a step forward, ready to donate four more dollars to the cause of solving the mystery.

Jack noticed the shift in my shadow. He quickly turned on me and bleated like an angry goat! I froze. It was a total head-slap moment for Sherlock.

I was the problem.

It wasn't that I was buying the wrong treat; it was that I was there in the first place. Jack had something going with this truck that had nothing to do with ice cream. I backed away a few steps to give him the space for whatever this was.

Satisfied that he had pushed me out of the "experience zone," Jack turned back to the truck. It was old and a little on the ratty side. It lumbered along our street, pushing the song ahead of it like a bulldozer.

"Yankee Doodle went to town,

Riding on a pony.

Stuck a feeauuutheeeer…"

As the truck went by, the music warped and pitched downward: The audio waves were now being dragged behind the truck.

Jack shrieked and jumped with delight. He looked at me, then back at the truck, then back at me again. He was checking to see if I finally understood. I was thunderstruck.

"Yes," I told him. "I heard it. That was amazing!"

And it was. This kid recognized pitch. He knew how the song should sound, and seemed to understand that the motion of the truck was distorting it. He'd figured this out without any language to help him reason through it. All summer long I'd thought ice cream was driving him to the curb: sugary, fatty, creamy and cold. But I had been projecting my own food passion onto my son. Jack's more cerebral passion diminished me.

He ran, jumped and flapped down the sidewalk after the truck, leaving me farther and farther behind. My opinion of him rose like a balloon.

"Truly amazing,"

7

Yeah, Sure! I'll Remember...

Please tell me it's not just me! All AutiMoms lose their memories, right? I figure it's the constant, extreme demand on our mental resources that causes a kind of selective cerebral burn-out. I say "selective," because not all memory is affected; just names, faces, locations, bits of conversation, why we went to the garage or opened a drawer, or ga-doy! Have you ever called someone on the phone then, by the time they answer, you forgot who you were calling? Can anything make you feel more ridiculous? Wait. Have I already asked you these questions?

Cards on the table: I wasn't the super-best at remembering names all my life. Or faces. In fact, back when I was twelve, I asked my sister to help me remember the name of a classmate, and I began describing this student. When my sister realized who I was talking about, she actually punched my arm! "What's wrong with you," she yelled. "Allison isn't blonde! She's taller than *you* are, and her eyes are green, not brown!" Yeah, that whole visual-memory thing was never my strong suit.

But I compensated with an audio-memory that was downright phonographic. I could replay in my head the entire soundtrack of a day, starting with the alarm going off (which made a faint "click" before the alarm started shrieking. I was terrified of the alarm and learned to wake up, jump out of bed and shut off the clock at the "click.") Then it was the scuff-scuff of slippers, the neighbor's dog barking twice, followed by a pause and a third bark, the slam-click of the bathroom door telling me a sister beat me to it, Mom calling down from the second floor, "Has anyone seen my car keys?" Bam! Pristine as the moment it all happened. This girl's got *memory*!

So what the heck happened?! Even if I couldn't always remember your name right away, I was an average, every-day social type. I'd meet you, we'd talk, and the next time I saw you, I could pick up right where we left off. "When does your boyfriend come back from Chicago?" "Double-expresso latte, right?" "Did you ever find out who stole your jacket?"

Things are different now, and that's why I'm wondering if it's just me. I'll be shopping or whatnot around town, and people will dash up to me waving and smiling! They're so happy to see me again, and I haven't a clue who the hell they are. I just stand there trapped by the honeydews hoping that something they say will trigger a memory, however fleeting. Usually it doesn't.

Or I'll get an email from school, "Just following up on that document we talked about. Could you send it over before noon today?" I mean, *come on*! Couldn't they have taken three extra seconds to type out the document's name?! So I'll spend 20 minutes going through old emails, looking for any mention of a document, all while hoping they hadn't asked me for it in person, because without a written record, I'm toast.

This happens to me a lot these days. I mean *a lot!* So much that

I can't really fake it anymore. I used to be all, "Hey, you, (because I can't remember your name)! Fancy meeting you here! (Now please respond with something that helps me remember where I know you from!)" But the empty banter isn't jumpstarting my memory like it once did, and people are starting to notice. They can tell my brain isn't shifting into gear.

That's how the melon encounter went south. In the middle of a long, utterly effervescent sentence, the woman paused, her eyes growing quizzical a moment. Then her face dropped. "You don't remember me, do you," she half-whispered, more to herself than to me. She was astonished. Our past encounter, whatever it was, had been deeply meaningful to her.

What could I say?! "Yeah, sort of…?"

We silently gazed at each other, half-smiling, inwardly grimacing. There was no place to go with this. She turned and walked back to the basket that she'd tossed aside near the deli.

You know that Hollywood cad who has doped-up, serial one night stands with fans and fledgling actresses, then in the morning gives them a fake phone number so they can "call him sometime?" Ahhhh! *I don't want to be that guy!!* But right then I totally felt like him! I even put the melons back and fast-walked out of the store for fear of running into the woman again on the cereal aisle!

If this is happening to you too, I know it's making you crazy!! What the heck is up with our brains?!

Well, I have a theory:

Our Kids Are Intoxicating

When I'm out with Jack, he has at least 60% of my attention at any time. Another ten percent is needed to keep me from tripping, walking into walls, or missing the chair as I sit. So if you're talking to me while I'm with Jack, you're getting the leftover 30%. Girl, I might as well be schnockered.

Seriously. Jack could be right there in my peripheral vision, and my brain will still be all: (Is Jack safe? Is he calm? Is he drawing attention to himself? How much longer is he likely to be patient?)

Suddenly I'll notice that I'm talking with some random adult. He's leaning in to make a point. "... in middle school, right? We all know what that's like! Ha-ha-ha!"

"Ha-ha-ha! (Who are you again? Someone just introduced us. Where'd they go? How long have we been talking?) Middle school, right... Don't get me started!"

"Exactly. So I told my wife that this was our last chance to move out of the school district before Madison would..."

...And I'm tuning out again. (What's Jack looking at? Is there an opportunity to teach him something? Can we practice a skill? What's happening nearby that I can engage him in?)

I know for a fact that I've walked away from people while they were still talking to me. I've purchased groceries, and then left the store with the bags still sitting at the check stand. I have introduced myself to the same person twice at a single event. These are things I *know* about! It frightens me to think how many others there must be: My skirt caught up in the waistband of my stockings, maybe? A curler still clinging to the back of my head? My phone left exposed on a table with my last text message lit-up: "So bored, just kill me!!"? I'm *glad* I don't know! I don't *want* to know!

But I suspect there's plenty of snickering 'round the water coolers all over town about "Jack's cognitive issues being *inherited* from his *mother*! Ha-ha-ha-ha."

Yeah?! Say that to my face, I dare you! I'd call you out on that right now! Except... I don't really know who you are. Or where I know you from. And if I run into you again somewhere, chances are I won't have a clue that we've ever met.

8

Duck, Duck, Bruise

Getting out of the house is a high-risk activity for any AutiMom.
We never know what might set our child off, when or where we
might be at the time, or how we'll be able to handle it without
abandoning our errands and slinking home in defeat. Even when
things are going well, some random stranger might still take offense
at something our children do that is so innocuous that we no
longer notice it. Then they butt in all huffy-like, and that in turn
sets off our kid.

Nothing. Pisses. Us. Off. More.

For example, maybe your kid is rocking back and forth in the
shopping cart, quietly saying, "Bang, bang, bang, bang…"
Suddenly some aging college student is within spittle-distance of
your face, preaching the evils of the NRA. And yes, that actually
happened to me.

Dude. I can handle my kid's disability,
but you need to handle your own.

At 18 months, Jack was a darling little rock-tosser. He'd amble along the banks of the man-made pond at our local park, squat down for a rock, then stand and chuck it far out into the water. It was so Andy Griffith, I could almost hear the whistling theme song.

Then one day Jack beaned a duck at 30 yards. Bam! Right on the noggin.

Immediately, an old hippie woman barreled down the bank towards us. My brain didn't pivot as fast as the situation did, and I stood there watching her charge. I was thinking, *Interesting. Hippie fashion doesn't work on women over 60: Straggly hair, long skirt and drooping bust line… she's kinda like a Brothers Grimm witch.*

Then she was in Jack's face, shrieking, cussing and whirling her bag of bread crumbs. That woke me up.

"Whoa, Broomhilda! You can't rush a toddler that you outweigh by 190 pounds! You want a fight? You pick it with me! And I've got pepper spray, so let's rumble!"

Okay, that was my fantasy speech. What I actually said was, "(nothing)" because Jack had it covered: He held his ground and shrieked back at the woman. And so…there they were, screaming at each other at increasingly loud volume.

Then the will of the hippie buckled. She went silent and retreated a step, startled, or perhaps chagrined. She glanced at me for help, but I just smiled and shook my head. *You turned to the wrong person, lady!*

Recognizing her defeat, she withdrew from the park, glaring back at us while spitting a hail of profanities.

Oh yeah! High five to the Jackster-Boy! Taking on the pond establishment!

But the pastime had suddenly lost its charm. This was not 1950's Mayberry; it was a man-made pond in a new-age park where the pecking order placed ducks above toddlers. Should I prevent Jack from tossing rocks? Should I constantly bodyguard him against further assault? I just wanted to relax, and now I couldn't.

On future park visits, I avoided the pond. When Jack's protests grew unbearable, I avoided the park altogether. So the ducks could relax, and the hippies were happy, but Jack was starved for his favorite game.

He began tossing rocks into every conceivable body of water – streams, swimming pools, fountains, bathtubs, puddles, sinks, fish tanks, rain buckets, bird baths, pet bowls, and yes, even the toilet. (I already had the plumber on speed-dial). Once at breakfast I took a grape off my plate and rolled it toward Jack to try. He picked it up and, with intense focus, dropped it into my coffee. Sigh.

I had to let this poor boy return to the pond.

I've come to believe that tossing rocks into water is more than an idle pass time. It's ear-math heaven for the audiophile. The size, width,

shape and density of the rock, combined with the force of the throw, the angle of descent and the depth of the water, all play a part in forming the sound the rock makes as it hits. "Blip," "blooop," "splat," "spa-looosh," the nearly silent knife-edge entry, and so on. The range of possible sounds is expansive. Judging by Jack's intense focus and delighted reactions, I suspect he knew the sound each rock would make before it hit the water. I can't do that. Can you?

This game also features visual math: Splash volume, wave height, wave spacing and ripple speed, all of which are harder to discern when you're stuck playing in a toilet bowl.

So, yes. It was a game worth risking the wrath of Broomhilda for. We resumed visiting the park pond several times a week for the next two years. I kept an eye out for our hippy friend, but she never returned. Jack may have scared her off for good.

Of course… she was replaced by others. The world seems to have an endless supply of hostile, insensitive people, and they tend to show up at the worst-possible moments. I don't know if these run-ins are the biggest problem AutiMoms face, but they are certainly one of the problems we talk about most when we're together. So I'm giving them their own chapter. They don't deserve it, but *we do*!

9

Going Off The Rails

You're not alone, okay? This has happened to all of us: You're stressed, you should've been done with (fill-in-the-blank) an hour ago, so the start-times on everything else for the rest of your day are shot. You might mentally downgrade dinner to takeout — that will help. But Errgh! Now your kiddo is wigging out in Walmart for reasons unknown and you're trying to keep damage to a minimum. A few jars got broken? You can live with it. As long as he doesn't knock down a whole display.

And of course, we've got to have people around you engaged in the usual staring, glaring, and just-pretend-he's-not-there-ing. Let's say this place has a manager that comes over to yell at you — because clearly you're not trying hard enough, right? Throw in a ringing cell phone just for fun. It sounds distant, because it's in your purse ... which you set on the floor over in the mustard section where the wig-out first started. Crap. It's now fully twelve strides away; almost another time zone. If you don't get to it in the next few minutes, it's pretty much fifty/fifty it will be stolen. Wallet, phone, keys, the lot.

This would be a really bad time for some stranger to get in your face; telling you what you're doing wrong, how to discipline your child, or why your child's on a one-way road to juvenile hall. This "helpful citizen" can't see your internal pressure gauge and doesn't know you're already well into the red. Back up, sweetheart. Mama's gonna blow.

And blown this mama has, with utter vesuvian flair. I try not to do it, I really do. But some people are so confident and self-aggrandizing that they will boldly wade into situations they know nothing about. Betty Buttinsky wants to be a busy body? Fine. There are plenty of opportunities out there for her to get her fill of self-importance. But this right here isn't one of them. Is she a doctor or therapist? No? Then she has no idea what she's looking at. So unless she wants to be sued for intentionally causing harm to a special needs child by disrupting his prescribed therapeutic intervention, she'd better get the hell out of here RIGHT NOW!

(Wow, good sentence! I might practice that one in front of a mirror! Ha-ha!)

Of course, these run-ins are not pretty. I'm not proud of them. I really do try to prevent them as much as possible. But when I can't, I also feel justified going a little psycho on these interlopers. Come on, girlfriend. We don't simply have an excuse to go loco, we have…

The Mother Of All Excuses

Here's the thing: We need incredible patience as we interact with our kids. We need to recognize a developing problem before it goes full-tilt. We need to know when and how to intervene, when to redirect, when to power through and when to let things settle out on their own. That's our job. It's a *big* job – so much bigger than it probably looks to those who've never done it. Plus, we don't get to clock out at 5:00pm. It's 24/7/365/for *life*.

What's *not* our job? Helping everyone else in the world mind their manners. If they can't stand politely back and let us do our job while our kids gnaw the paint off the door of their new car, *they're* the problem, not us! And if they're not careful, they might get kicked right between the old *ojos*.

I'm not suggesting we go around looking for *ojos* to kick. But! If people can't see that we're already hanging by a thin thread when they take out their scissors and start snipping at us just because they find our presence annoying, maybe they have it coming.

Plus there's this: If people can rob a bank or throw bricks through someone's windows or stand buck-naked on the Dumbarton Bridge screaming, "I'm Henry the VIII," or what-have-you, and then get off Scott free by claiming temporary insanity? Come on! Do you see what I'm saying? *Our whole life* is insane! AutiMotherhood is the Mother of all excuses!

Once we embrace our inner psycho-bitch, the clouds will part and birds will line our path to serenade us as we the stride the world in our Bubble of Awesome. That kind of freedom is exhilarating!

But...

It's also a little frightening, let's be honest. When you're way out there in the wide open where there are no fences to hold you back, there's nothing holding you in, either. Everyone needs fences. Otherwise your cows will separate and start roaming every which way, getting lost, rustled, and eaten by wolves. (Sorry. Colorado's getting to me.) You might want to figure how much latitude for crazy you want to have, then put down a nice solid perimeter beyond which you simply will not go.

The perimeter is different for all of us; our kids are different, our normal temperaments are different and the communities we live in are different. My New York City friends claim max latitude, for example. My friends in L.A. are stuck competing against local crazies, so they have to amp it up just to be noticed. Here in the Rockies, we're more reserved. "Boring," as some might say. But I have formed my Perimeter of Crazy by using five principles which I'm happy to share in case you need a little jump-start in forming your own:

1. I will not be the one who starts anything.
Because crap happens all the time, right? Say I'm strolling up to the park with my son and he stops to flap-and-gasp at the pedestrian crossing sign. He loves that thing for some reason. It's interesting to him. So I take a seat nearby and let him do his thing. Then a couple of eight year olds on Barbie bikes stop to ask Fifty Questions. "What's wrong with him?" "Why does he like this sign?" "Why is he panting? Can't he breathe?" "Is he stupid?" "Is he going to die?" *You first you little brat!*

Are they being rude? Yes! But they're eight years old. So they're not really *starting* anything. Neither is the guy who crosses to the other side of the street while passing us, then crosses back. (*Snort.* Did he think we wouldn't see that cross-back?)

If Barbie Bikes' mom runs up to nervously shoo the girls away with, "Let's not bother the nice lady," *she's* not starting anything either. But if, instead, she says, "You really should keep that kid at home," — which yes, someone has actually said to me — *now* she's in my target zone.

2. I will give people a second chance.

When someone seems to jump in all ugly right from the get-go, odds are something's awry. Most people don't generally do that. When they do, it's often because they have their own issues going on that I may want to map out before letting loose on them. Ticking off someone who's already quasi-postal and who might follow me home with an axe and a grudge is not on my bucket list.

More likely, it's a misunderstanding. For example, that stranger didn't actually say, "Get that damn (r-word) out of my sight," he said "Let that *ham discard* fall to the right." See? Who wants their ham discards falling leftward? So it's good to let him clear that up. Or say a strange woman charges at us screaming, "You A-holes are driving me crazy," I will look to see if I'm standing in front of a mobile proctology clinic. Because, who knows, right? A polite, "Are you talking to us," may be all I need to turn the interaction onto a friendly path.

3. I will try not to lose complete control.

I have in the past, as you'll soon see, and it's left me feeling like a scum-ball, tongue-tied reprobate for weeks afterwards. Yippee. So I truly fight against it. Instead, I'll push back with whatever force the situation calls for, using anger just as a tool. The goal isn't to hurt, it's to rebalance. As soon as there's a break in the other person's aggression, the situation is over. It's important I be ready (and able) to throttle back. I figure anything that happens past that point is on me.

4. I will accept an apology in the spirit given

Which means, if it's sarcastically given, it will be accepted with sarcasm. That's pretty rare, though. Most apologies are sincere, and I want to be quick to accept them so the other guy knows I'm not holding a grudge. People will often feel horrible on the back side of an argument with the mother of a disabled child. And I mean H.O.R.R.I.B.L.E! The relief they find in your forgiveness will change the course of their whole day. They may even wind up becoming an ally.

5. I will keep my child away from the fight

Usually Jack is so engrossed with whatever he's doing that he has no idea it's causing a fight. That frees me to take on all comers like Bruce Lee — Punch, kick, twirl, double-kick, back-flip, *ha!* As long as Jack is unbothered by the scuffle, I'm golden. But as soon as he shows any sign of distress, I wrap it up — even if the other guy is in the middle of a 40 stanza Ode to Insulting my Mother.

So yeah, this isn't some Award-Winning Tip-a-palooza: You're probably doing most of these things on your own already. But thinking everything through and having it all organized and settled in my mind before getting into a tussle has made a big difference for me. Because, True Story: Back when Jack was about three and I was new to AutiMotherhood, I went through a period of maybe six months when I was terrified to leave the house. People gave me so much flak everywhere we went! Getting a sitter was arduous — my "victims" would take the job once, then swipe my subsequent calls right into voice mail. My family was all out of state. I was trapped. So I responded by trapping myself even further by holing up in the house, shopping on line, eating delivery sandwiches, and tip-toing to the mailbox in the dead of night. I was afraid of my son, afraid of the public, and afraid of how angry I was starting to feel. I hope this does not sound familiar to you, because it was awful. Just in case, I've ordered an extra shot of tequila for your marg.

Having a ready perimeter for crazy has helped me big time. I now feel comfortable going forth in the world, and can keep myself reasonably civilized as I battle the Buttinskies. You know, deep down inside most Buttinskies are civilized, too. We can't blame everyone for the insensitivity of some.

But there *are some*. And sadly, among that "some" are a tiny few who will see your child's meltdown as an opportunity to launch their own social media stardom. I think we all agree that these people are the scum- "some." They are video bullies, and bullies need to be taken down (after making sure said bully isn't a bonafide psychopath). However! Stepping up to yell at them or smack their phone from their hands will serve their interests more than yours, because they can now include your angry reaction in their video. You might wind up with a lovely visit from Child Protective Services thanks to that YouTube VIP-wannabe. Meanwhile, I discovered a trick that has worked fantastic in each of the few situations I've needed it. You might put this in your back pocket with fingers crossed that you will never have to use it:

If someone starts filming me or my child I will pull out my own cell phone and film back at them. I don't make eye contact; I keep

my gaze on the screen whenever my eyes are not on my child. And! (This is important.) **I don't say a word**. Silence is a powerful weapon; it puts people off balance. Usually they'll start talking to fill the void. And they'll talk and talk and talk until they hear how mean and childish they sound. No one wants to sound that way on their own video, so they stop filming. Then they realize they sound just as awful on *my* video — which I continue to silently film. That's typically when they walk away, with or without some parting profanity.

Okay, that was fun. Bye-bye now.

I'm going to have a few stories here where I admittedly went Off The Rails. I'll flag them with the PsychoMom illustration so you can skip past them if you like. Let me say that I'm not... uhh... *proud* of the stories that fall into this category. Grown-ups are supposed to control themselves better than this. But the people who got the situation rolling in the first place are *also grown-ups*! Grown-ups who were guilty of being:

A) Rude

B) Selfish

C) Unkind

D) Aggressive

E) Ignorant

F) Bossy   yes!

G) Impossible to Ignore!!!

Until they learn to control *themselves* we may be doing a favor to society at large by cracking open the occasional can of whoop-ass. So. I have no plans of changing my ways. If that makes me a bad person, go ahead and hand me the badge. But please tell friends and family to buy my book anyway. I may need the money for bail.

10

Welterweight Mailboxing

Our first run-in with a rabid adult happen when Jack was not quite two years old. Until then, I had no idea people could be so ugly in front of a child, and as you will see, I was not yet seasoned at sass-back.

Let me set the scene: Jack had started talking at 13 months, and then he stopped. Shocker, right? Most of us share the same story. But Jack's medical team assumed his *hearing* was to blame. They spent the next 10 months running audiology tests in order to pinpoint the problem. Autism wouldn't enter the discussion for another year.

Meanwhile, Jack and I spent our afternoons walking the neighborhood. I was studying sign language and now used it whenever possible as I followed his meanderings along the route. "Rock." "Fence." "Butterfly." "Bike."

And, "Mailbox," wry laugh. We lived in one of those older neighborhoods where everyone still had a personal mailbox at the end of their driveway. Each box was different: a birdhouse, a mail truck, a cow… total postal anarchy. Jack touched each box he passed, lifting their flags, pushing the flags back, opening their doors and closing them again. Here I came, right behind him, signing and saying, "Mailbox, mailbox, mailbox," helping him generalize how these items, which all looked so different, were actually the same thing.

The street through our neighborhood snaked around a municipal open space, and then curved up the hill toward the University. It had a wild, pine-forest feel to it that encouraged residents to lounge in their front yards with the chipmunks and woodpeckers. Everyone knew us, although none of us knew each other by name. There was the guy with the fake deer among his scrub oak that Jack liked to pet. There was the flower-garden lady (her yard had bees, so Jack would run past it in a panic), and the guy with the three pick-up trucks parked on a gravel landing; one red, one white and one blue. Booyah. The house by the crosswalk was rented to a gaggle of nursing school students, and next door to them was a lady who went all-out on seasonal decorations twelve months a year: Valentine's, St. Patrick's Day, Veterans' Day... She did it all. It was a perfect neighborhood for a two year old to explore.

Well, *almost* perfect.

Halfway along our walk sat a house that was continuously being renovated — to the point where you gotta wonder why the owner didn't just buy a different house to begin with! First he added a second story. Then he widened the front door and attached a wrap-around porch. The house façade was redone in stone and clapboard, and now the lawn was being replaced with boulders and aspen trees. The owner did much of the work himself, accompanied by his two young sons who strutted around beside him, acting busy. They were probably four and six that summer. Every now and then I would stop and tell the owner how nice the house was looking and he would use that opportunity to brag about the work under way. So even though he didn't "know me" *know* me — not invite-me-to-his-barbeque *know* me — he *knew* me. There was no excuse for this story to have ever happened.

On the fateful day, we moseyed along the walk with Jack opening and closing each mailbox, and me saying and signing, "Mailbox," so... basically the same as every other day. But this time Renovation Man jumped off his new wrap-around porch and charged toward the sidewalk. Six and four year old Frick and Frack  followed after him. "What are you doing," asked Reno-Man.

"Yeah! What are you doing," asked Frick.

"What are you doing," asked Frack, pointing a finger at me that was still chubby with baby fat.

All three of them had sleeveless white t-shirts on. It was almost comical, and I almost laughed. "We're walking the neighborhood."

Reno-Man wasn't having it. "No you're not! You're going through people's mail!"

"Where'd you get that idea?"

"I watched you coming down the street! Opening every mailbox!"

"Give me a break. The mailman hasn't even come by yet."

"You don't know that!"

Did he seriously not recognize me? "Yes, I do. I live right around that curve!"

"Mail tampering is a felony," countered Reno-Man.

"Yeah," yelled Frick.

"Mail stamping our baloney," yelled Frack.

We were passing the point where someone could back off and

maybe pretend they were kidding. Reno-Man and his kids were torqueing each other up. "What is your problem," I asked, pointing at my son. "He's two!"

"You're not! You could go to jail for this!" Reno-Man unsnapped a holster on his belt, pulled something out and thrust it at my face. Adrenaline flooded my veins as I assumed I was about to be shot. But it was his phone. "Whaddya say I call the police! Right now! Huh? Huh?" He shoved the phone closer to prove he was serious.

Fueled by adrenaline, I slapped his phone away so hard that it damn-near buried itself into the freshly tilled soil of his yard.

"You want to call the police? Do it, tough guy! Or are you so tough? You had to drag your toddlers along to be your back-up! Do you always do that when you confront scary felons? Bring your toddlers?" I mocked him by shoving my empty hand into his face. "Maybe I should be the one calling *Child Protective Services!* Huh? Huh?" Pretending to make a call I continued, "Hey, Officer! This guy throws his kids in the path of people he thinks are felons! Maybe you should take his kids away! Oh, and by the way? Check out his front yard. See the plastic toys lying around right alongside the electric saws and nail guns? 'Gee, Billy. Should we play catch

today, or should we drive nails into each other's skulls?' 'Aw, Bobby. I'd rather saw off some fingers!'" I guess I didn't need the fake phone anymore? I didn't know what I was doing, but I was on a roll. "What kind of father are you? You're a danger to your children, that's what! Probably a danger to all of us! In addition to just being *totally f_ _king insane!*" And that's where I ran out of words.

We stood there staring at each other until we both became aware of a faint, "Squeak… squoke. Squeak… squoke."

Jack was still opening and shutting Reno-Man's mailbox.

Reno-Man looked back at me with a "what-the-hell" expression just in time for me to finish him off. "He's deaf, asshole!"

His face went from red to gray; mortified, hopefully, but still too proud to apologize. "Well… get him away from my mailbox."

"With pleasure! I wouldn't want him running across your porn magazines!"

(Okay, that was too much.)

I picked up Jack and closed the mailbox door. I was shaking with anger and wanted to flee, but I didn't know which way to step: Were we continuing on our walk? Should I cross the street, *then* continue our walk? Should I turn back and go home?

The day was ruined.

I started for home, tears flowing.

Reno-Man's day was ruined, too, of course. He shooed his boys towards the big porch. He would never speak to us again — his loss; one less neighbor he could brag to about his home. (Snort!) He was a big-ass jerk who only yelled at us because he'd finished his house and now wanted to remake the whole damn neighborhood! Thinking that made me feel better.

But he was right, too. Mail theft was real. Jack's hobby might have made a lot of our neighbors uncomfortable, and Reno-Man could have been the only one bold enough to say so. I tried not to sob. There were so few things Jack was interested in doing, and now one of them would have to stop.

In the distance, I heard Frick's voice asking, "Dad! What's a porn magazine?"

Women were not meant to have children after age 30

You had your first period at, what, age 11? That's nature telling you that you're ripe. By 30, you're starting to wrinkle and get a few gray hairs. That's nature telling you that you're past your "Best Used By" date.

Or so the argument goes.

This piece of folksy wisdom was passed on to me by a family member. I'm not going to name any names here, but sheesh. Is it possible to fire your family?

11

You're Fired!

Don't get me wrong: Families are great. Some AutiMoms have the most amazing families, who babysit, ask questions, read up on the latest treatments, and help cover some of the exorbitant cost of raising an AutiKid. If that describes you, uh… the rest of us hate you, by the way. Most AutiMoms have families that leave us feeling somewhere between "Meh," and "Quit tracking me down!" If that sounds more like you, then you may have been subjected to the aforementioned Weird Autism Myth #2.

The point of that myth is to allow the people around you to blame *you* for your child's disability. "You caused this, it's your problem, don't expect us to help you fix it." It doesn't, however, prevent this family member type from offering you tons of advice. After all:

- ☑ It costs them nothing,

- ☑ Any schadenfreude guilt they may feel is salved by this generous act of "charity,"

- ☑ They get to pretend they're smarter than you, and

- ☑ You are relegated to the diminished status of Knowledge-Welfare Recipient.

Cool! Who doesn't want all that?! Plus, it sets the stage for future status readjustments when you experience ongoing problems after not exercising their advice to some *impossible specificity*. After all, the advice is never faulty. *You* must be doing something *wrong*!

Totally made-up example: "Did you use a spoon to stir the bath salts into the water, like I told you? Don't get lazy and just stir the water with your hand... You did? Okay, not a plastic spoon (sniff), it has to be metal. It is? Wait, not one of those big spoons you keep in your kitchen for eating ice cream (because you're such a selfish, ice cream-eating fatty, but I'm not saying that directly)... Oh, you bought a new spoon just for this? Good. That's good... Well, is the handle blue? No? *There's* your problem. The handle has to be blue or the bath therapy isn't going to work."

Sigh.

Every member of my family lives half a country away, so I can't say how ugly things might have gotten between us. Judging by the average AutiMom Club Member's experience, however, "Pretty ugly," sounds reasonable.

Some people don't adjust well to having an AutiChild in the family tree – particularly older relatives. Plus there's the tendency within families to say crap that nobody else in their right mind would say. When that happens, you're stuck either submitting to the abuse, leaving the room, or standing firm and blowing up the family bond.

It's your choice, and trust me: I will not judge you. There *is* a theory, however, that autism runs in families. You could always point to the offending relative and say, "Gee. You must be the carrier of the cognitive disability gene." Boom. Curtsy. Exit.

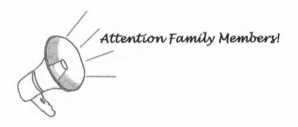

Attention Family Members!

If you want to show you care, ask questions! Don't hold forth with info you heard or read somewhere. We are <u>living</u> this, so chances are pretty good we know more than you already!

The thing is, you've got too much to do right now and too many decisions to make to be sidetracked by ridiculous "bath salt cures," or winged by a family member looking to inflict a grudge-wound.

Wow, did I just say "grudge-wound?"

Oh yeah, girlfriend.

The family's reaction to any life change in a member of that family is never "pure." It doesn't matter what the change is:

- ☑ Getting a juicy job offer in London
- ☑ Quitting said juicy job (or better yet, being fired)
- ☑ Starting a business
- ☑ Filing for bankruptcy
- ☑ Getting married
- ☑ Getting divorced
- ☑ Winning the lottery

- ☐ Becoming a mother

- ☐ Having a child diagnosed with autism

The family's reaction to any big news is tangled up in a snarl of issues they already have with you. They may still be ticked at you for being Aunt Myrtle's favorite, or that you got straight "A"s in school without trying, or that you used to beat them in tennis. Maybe they never got over the fact that you bleached your hair in college, or that when the whole neighborhood was evacuated during a brush fire, you were the only one that was interviewed by the TV news crew. A lot of us run smack into grudges that we didn't know were there. Your disabled child could be serving as a handy vehicle for family members to vent some pent-up beef they have that goes back to when you were three and flushed your sister's goldfish down the toilet. Seriously. Petty. Garbage.

If you can muscle your way past the grudges and rebuild a supportive family that will help you now when you need it most, that's fantastic and highly worthwhile. If you can't, that's okay too. Sometimes you just have to fire your family in order to focus on the job ahead. Your workload won't be this heavy forever. In five to ten years, you can always reconnect with your family.

Unless that goldfish thing remains an issue.

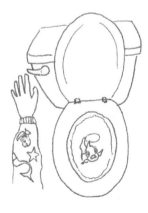

Now, here's the deal: We're not the only ones with junk in our life that leaves us feeling miserable. Our kids do, too. They need to "fire" that stuff to regain their mental equilibrium just as much as we do. Perhaps more so. But because they have autism, they may go about this in odd ways, and if you're like me, you may not recognize what you're looking at when you first see it.

Byyyyyyye Wooooooooody!

When Jack was three-going-on-four, he had a Sheriff Woody doll that went everywhere with him. He liked looking at it, pulling its string, and listening to the cowboy drawl of its recorded phrases. But mostly he liked the way Sheriff Woody felt in his hand. It had a light, floppy body, and its head, hands and feet were heavy—total

killer combination! The smallest toss would send those heavy limbs outward in a star formation, and Woody would fling through the air – going much farther than the toss deserved. Oh-ho-ho, *yeah!!*

Yeaaaaaah....

That was the year I bought my first grab-nabber.

Woody wound up in trees and bushes, on the edges of roofs, on the tops of trucks and playground structures, down sewer drains, on balconies and ledges, and I can't remember where-all. But I do remember strolling around the neighborhood with Jack and thinking, for example, "Gee, I hope he doesn't throw Woody over that fence." Then bingo! Woody would go flying over precisely that fence. I'm pretty sure our kids can read minds.

Jack would then silently turn to me with utterly innocent expectation, reaching toward wherever Woody had gone – his face could melt my iciest mood. So, I'd pull the grab-nabber out of my bag and go Woody-fishing. I was actually pretty good at it; partially climbing trees, hanging over fences, jumping and snatching at rooflines —not a real resume ornament, but it helped keep me in shape.

Sheriff Woody was thrown pretty much everywhere over the course of that year, so when I found him one day, tangled up in the bushes on the hill behind our home, I didn't give it a thought. I plucked Woody out and returned him to his regular spot on top of Jack's bookshelf.

Later that same day, Woody was back out on the hill.

Well now, what?

Jack had just gotten up from his nap, so when-the-heck had he gone outside, and how did he get out there without me? The sliding glass door in the back of our house was a beast! Plus, I kept a wooden dowel parked in its tracks to thwart burglars. How was Jack not equally thwarted?

Lifting the dowel and heaving the door open, I stepped out on the deck and gave the back hill a good eye-squint. Yep, that was Woody; splayed like a starfish across a bed of goats-head weed. Luckily he hadn't been spotted and snatched by some child (or pet) wandering along the greenbelt. I crossed the grass, picked Woody up and brushed away the stickers. On the second floor of our house, Jack was visible through his room window. He was standing in front of his computer, flapping happily. Video games; he could play them for hours.

So... when was he *out here?*

I carried the toy back into the house, and with it, the Big Scary Thought that all parents of special needs kids eventually have:

My child could run off, get lost and be unable to communicate with anyone trying to help. Or worse...

Time to deploy defensive counter-thoughts:

Jack's Sheriff Woody toy is still on the bookcase; this one belongs to another kid.

(...who also happened to leave it on the hill behind our home? Really?)

Wait! No! I meant to get Woody off the hill earlier, but I never actually did it.

(And the toy moved from the bush to the ground on its own. Yepper-do.)

It was in the open space! It could have been moved by a wild animal!

(Check. So when Jack runs off, he will also come face-to-face with wild animals: Coyotes, bears, mountain lions, maybe a rattle snake...)

The defensive counter-thoughts weren't working.

I bounded the stairs two at a time and entered Jack's room where I found the bookshelf to be utterly Woody-free — of course it was. I crossed the room and placed the sheriff in his designated spot.

Jack was so engrossed in his game that he didn't see me come in. I stood a moment, admiring the back of his curly, blonde head. He needed a haircut. The curls bounced as he attacked the mouse and backed away. Victory over the game caused him to squeal. Such a beautiful kid. But my thoughts slid back into darkness: A mountain lion could sneak around behind Jack as easily as I just had. We needed elopement locks on our doors *today*.

It became my mission.

I went down to the kitchen and opened my laptop. While it booted, I put a cup of coffee into the microwave and pulled up a stool to the counter. Googling "Elopement Prevention," I clicked a link for "Special Needs Elopement Packages" and scanned the page for actionable intel:

- **GPS Trackers!**
- **Keyless Door Locks!**
- **Medical Alert Bracelets!**
- **Seatbelt Guards!**
- **Over-the-door deadbolts!**
- **Video surveillance systems!**
- **And So Much More!**

Shesh! Who could afford all this stuff?! Would the deadbolt alone be enough in our case?

I needed a shopping Sherpa!

I picked up my phone to text Jack's behavioral therapist. She might know exactly what Jack needed.

Behind me the microwave beeped, which I ignored, but… I heard something else, too: Footsteps directly above me. I looked up and tracked the path of these steps as they padded toward the back of the house. This was followed by a sound that was jarringly "adult:"

Click, whuuuummmp.

Through the sliding glass door, I now saw Woody cartwheeling through the air. The toy bounced once as it hit the back hill.

Whuuuummmp. Click.

The footsteps returned to the center of the ceiling. Jack had learned to open his window!

Hey Kids! Why settle for being mauled by a wild animal when you can first fall from a second story window? Yaaaaaaaay!

"Oh. My. God."

Back on the web page, I dove to the "magnetic window alarms" link and clicked through to begin absorbing the options. Seriously; I could be as monomaniacal as Jack. Meanwhile, the microwave continued to beep at me every 30 seconds. (Hey! Your coffee is ready! Hey! I said, your coffee is ready!) This intermittent snag on my focus eventually pried me loose, and I was able to wake up to the importance of this moment:

Jack had thrown his favorite toy out the window!

In a way, Woody had been Jack's first "best friend." This was a break-up, as hard emotionally as any break-up with a real friend. The window latches could wait. I closed the laptop and went up the stairs.

Jack was deep into his game again and didn't look over as I sat against the edge of his desk. This time, however, he knew I was there. I didn't want to cause him any more distress than he was already feeling, so I chose the fewest words possible. "No more Woody?"

"No more Woody," He confirmed, continuing his play.

But why? Did a kid yelled at Jack while Jack was playing with Sheriff Woody? Did a mean kid have his own "mean" Sheriff Woody? Did Jack have a bad dream about the toy? He couldn't tell me of course. But I was certain that something ugly happened, and now whenever Jack looked at Woody, he remembered this ugly thing. The only way to get rid of that ugly memory was to get rid of Woody. So, out the window he went. Mood-management at its purist.

"Okay then," I said. "No more Woody." I stroked his hair to assure him it really was "okay."

The Urge to Purge

Woody was surely not the first beloved item Jack had fired from his life. A Tigger bath toy — which, when Jack was two-and-a-half, I thought would have to be surgically removed from his fist — simply vanished one day. A few months later, his favorite DVD went missing, and I scoured the house for it in a panic. Both times, Jack was oddly ambivalent. With 20/20 hindsight, it's now clear what was up, but it wasn't until the ignominious defenestration of Sheriff Woody that the lightbulb went on over my head.

Now I saw it regularly: A favorite book was found stuffed in the trash. A favorite food item was pulled from the lunch box and left on the counter, several days running. The unclogging of a toilet produced one of Jack's favorite shirts. Once, while we were driving along, Jack abruptly ejected a music CD and flung it out the window.

This need to physically purge negative thoughts from his life continued well into his teens —even after he'd begun speaking and was better equipped to grapple with thought. So… like any good mother observing a trend, I considered Jack's urge to purge and developed a family-wide strategy: I made it a holiday.

Happy Good Riddance Day!

The night before New Year's Eve my family celebrates Good Riddance Day by sitting at a table littered with colored paper and colored markers. Grabbing a sheet and a pen, we each write down one thing that we are glad to get rid of as the year comes to a close: Bad friends, bad classes, getting stranded with a flat tire while we were on vacation, a broken toe, a savage hailstorm that broke our back windows, the obnoxious neighbors that moved away, the night a bear climbed onto our deck, that disastrous haircut, the burnt toast that set off the smoke alarms; you name it. We write down one item per sheet, and ceremoniously carry it over to the shredder while loudly announcing "Goodbye burnt toast that set off our smoke alarms!" Everyone cheers and goes on to the next item.

We typically start kind of slow, shredding only those things that really nagged at us. After a while, though, the fun of the shredding begins to infect us, and before you know it, we're shredding a broken Fit Bit, that off-brand deodorant mom thought we might like, the woodpecker that finally stopped pecking the back of our house, the time that guy at the drive-thru forgot to put fries in our bag… until no negative is too unshreddably small. It's a lot of fun! Once we're done, we take the shredder bucket outside and throw fistfuls of colored shreds into the wind like confetti! Good riddance! Good riddance to it all!

Life is full off minor indignities. You suffered plenty

of them before your spectrum child was born. But

now, oh ho! Now the indignities are pro-class, heavy

weight, major league, and occurring daily. Stand

tall, mama. Be proud. You can take it.

12

What's That Smell?

Sensory Processing Disorder is like a small sucker fish clinging to the side of the shark of autism. Thank you. Yes. I'm great with useless visuals. At any rate, most of our kids have SPD, or had it, or will have it at some point in their development. For whatever reason, it seems to come and go. It's enough to drive a mom crazy — especially when you have to explain it to someone who is "thoughtfully sharing" some advice she got from a yoga blog (or whathaveyou). And you know… most people don't really get "medical speak." They'll nod like their listening, but they're really just waiting for you to pause so they can start talking about that yoga post again.

The good news is: Over the course of a good 100 conversations, I've cobbled together a description of Sensory Processing Disorder that any non-med-speak-speaking human can understand!

Sensory Processing Disorder For Dummies

BY JACK'S MOM

Imagine you're catching a baseball. You see the ball coming toward you until it meets your glove. You hear the ball smack against the leather. You feel the weight and velocity of the ball's arrival in your hand. It all happens smoothly together. You close your glove, and the ball is caught.

But if you have SPD, those three sensory signals don't arrive to your brain at the same time. You might hear the smack of leather first, and separately see the ball meet the glove. Only then might you feel the ball punch into your hand. A whiff of cut grass might muscle its way into the lineup somewhere to demand its own brain-time, even though it has nothing to do with catching. When are you supposed to close the glove? Has the ball arrived yet? Did you already drop it? You simply can't tell.

You're welcome.

Seriously. I endured 100 idiotic recommendations for "fixing" my child in order to come up with this analogy. Please go out and use it!

Jack went through a period where his most "dysintegrated sense" — the one separated farthest from the others— was smell. And the more separated a sense is, the larger it seems to loom in the head. Yeah. This is probably what drives our kids to burrow themselves into sand or shriek when you open a mayonnaise jar or cover their ears near an escalator. Your kiddo probably has his own odd thing that he does. It's cool; there's no shame in the AutiMom Club. Jack's thing was hunting down and labeling the world's odors.

He was six years old at the time, and still three years away from functional speech, but he was able to ask, "What's that smell?" He said it a lot, especially around visitors, or when we were visiting others, or when we were speaking to people in public. If I had a buck for every mortified look on the face of an unsuspecting stranger… I might not be a millionaire, but I'd have a solid down-payment on a new car!

Jack went sniffing through crowds like a drug-enforcement K-9. It wasn't always pit-stench and garlic-breath that stopped him. Sometimes it was the smell of new shoes, or a lycra girdle warming up under someone's dress, or the whiff of sesame oil that somebody's jacket picked up last week at a Chinese restaurant. Not subtle enough? How about if it's not coming from the person in front of us at all! How about if it's coming from someone popping a Tic Tac three checkstands away? I'm not kidding! Wintergreen or Cinnamon Spice?

So of course I had to look this up in the middle of the night. Our children drive us to learn all kinds of stuff that we never would have otherwise been curious about. The official term for Jack's sniff-o-mania is "hyperosmia." And this is the story of how it got me stuck in an elevator.

Up and Down

Twice a week Jack went in for customized allergy shots in a four-story medical building. (Yes, he was allergic to everything! I could write a full book on this alone!) The allergist was on the ground floor. The door to her practice was right beside a small elevator. One day, as I was signing Jack in at the front desk and chit-chatting casually with Joan, the receptionist, I noticed Jack was no longer beside me. Insta-panic. As I searched in a frantic 360, several people in the waiting area pointed in unison to the door.

"(Expletive deleted)!"

I dashed back out to the lobby just in time to see the doors closing on the small elevator. There he was. He saw me, gave me a grin/flap combo, and then disappeared beyond the doors. I lunged into the call button, but I was too late. The car began ascending. I would have to beat him up the stairs. I kicked off my high heels and started running.

I heard the elevator "ding" as I hit the mid-floor landing. By the time I got to the second floor, the doors had opened and were now closing. Jack saw me running towards him and squealed with delight. The closing doors then separated us. The car began whirring upwards again. I ran back to the stairs.

Once again the elevator "dinged" before I got past the landing. When I reached the 3rd floor, Jack was leaning out the doors looking for me. I paused at the top of the stairs long enough for our eyes to meet and for him to squeal. But I was on to this racket, now: I had to keep climbing or I'd miss again on the next floor.

I took the final flight 2 stairs at a time and was charging across the fourth floor lobby as the elevator "dinged." The doors were just starting to open when I leaped through.

"Gotcha!"

Jack's scream dissolved into loud laughter. Everyone in the building probably heard it. We stood in the elevator a moment while he laughed and I caught my breath. Jack was six, as I mentioned, and I was still coupling sign language with speech for him. After we rested, I signed and said, "Okay. Time to go back." I punched the first floor button and the doors closed. We descended to the 2nd floor where the car stopped.

We should have gotten off and walked down that final flight of stairs.

"Let's stay on," I told Jack, signing and pointing to the floor indicator. "We're on '2' and we need to go to '1.'"

That's when I noticed the sudden turn in Jack's mood. He had an odd look on his face, like he was thinking hard about something unpleasant.

The doors opened. Two people in radiology scrubs stepped towards us: A female with an ultrasound badge, and a male sporting a badge from X-ray. Together they may have weighed 450lbs. I guided Jack to the side to give them room to board. Jack barely looked at them.

As the second radiologist stepped in, the elevator bounced slightly and issued five high-pitched beeps. I didn't mean to glance at them – like I was accusing them of being too heavy to ride this small elevator together (plus, I need to lose a pound or twenty myself, so I who am I to throw the first scone?) — But… there I was glancing the heck out of them. Ultrasound Girl swished her hand at me. "Nothing to worry about," she said, smiling. "It does that sometimes."

Then Jack said, "What's that smell?" Great timing, right? The radiologists now thought they'd been called both fat *and stinky.* "What's that smell?!" Jack looked up at me.

"I don't smell anything," I said and signed, forcing a smile to ease any potential social discomforts. But the fact was, I actually *didn't* smell anything. The doors began to close.

Jack turned to stare at the gap where the doors slid in and out. "What's that smell," he demanded. And just before the doors shut, he slipped out of the car.

"Jack!"

The doors bounced shut, leaving a half-inch space between them. I could see a thin sliver of Jack standing beyond. "Jack, stay right there!" I triple-punched the door-open button, hoping to get off before the car began moving, but it was too late. The visible sliver of Jack appeared to glide upward. I yelled, "Stay there, Jack! I'll come right back!" Of course, he couldn't see me signing. The likelihood that he understood me was zero.

But wait: It gets worse.

The elevator jolted and made a kind of jack-hammering sound. Then it lost all power: Lights, motion, fan; everything went out — including my brain. *This did not just happen!* Through the door-gap, Jack's feet were at my eye level.

"Does it do this sometimes, too," I asked my co-riders. The bitchy sarcasm in my voice surprised me.

I was more surprised by the breathless response: "No!"

I looked over at Ultrasound Girl. Her face was panicked. She had one hand flat against the wall and the other gripping the X-ray Guy's shoulder. He didn't look so hot either. I'm not proud of the fact that I blamed these two for causing whatever just happened, and their reactions now were beyond irritating. "We're fine," I snapped. "The doors are ajar, we have plenty of air. We have enough light. We're halfway to the ground floor. The worst we can fall is six feet."

"There's a basement," moaned X-ray.

"Listen to me. Do you see that?" I pointed upward at Jack's legs. "That's our problem! He's special needs and he's by himself! *He's* the one that's in danger!"

"Try the intercom," I barked.

X-ray stepped to the control panel and squinted at the dark buttons.

"Hi Jack," I called sweetly up through the doors, hoping the sound of my voice would encourage him to stay put. "I'm still here! I don't know if I'm going up or going down. Thank you for waiting for me. Stay right there, okay?"

"Hello?" X-ray leaned into the panel. "Hello? Can anyone hear me? We're stuck in the elevator!"

I dug around my purse for my cell phone.

"I'm getting nothing," X-ray said. "I think the intercom's dead."

Ha-ha-ha... yeah. Listen, I'm a good, caring person. Someone's five bucks short at the checkout stand? I'll cover it for them. A neighbor break her leg? I'll bring her flowers and a homemade meal. But maybe I'm a *part-time bitch*. Because when I'm with Jack, all my compassion and concern is funneling toward him. There's nothing left for anyone else. And really, are other adults *that* incapable of taking care of themselves?

"OH MY GOD," screamed Ultrasound Gal as she began pounding on the doors and shrieking. And I mean ear-piercingly. "HELP! PLEASE! SOMEONE HELP US!"

The visible sliver of Jack's leg shifted, then disappeared.

"Jack!"

I turned to Ultrasound, and if she could have scanned an image of my mind right then, she would have quit her job in horror. "Knock it off! You just drove my son away!"

"I'm trying to get help!" She was scared to the point of sweating. I'd feel sorry for her later, but right then I wanted to punch her.

"How does a grown woman freaking out *help anything*?! If my son runs out into the parking lot and gets hit by a car, I swear to god!"

The sound of my voice may have been scarier than the idea of plummeting down the elevator shaft. She froze mid-pound, staring at me.

"Get away from the door! Go! Stand in the corner there! I don't want to hear a god damn peep out of you!"

She backed herself into the far corner. I brought the allergist's number up on my cell phone and called the front desk.

"Pine Ridge Aller…"

"Joan, this is Jack's mom. I'm sorry to be short, but I need your help. I'm stuck on the elevator, and Jack is loose in the building. Can you please make sure he doesn't run out the front doors?"

"Oh! We were looking for you! Would you… should I call Maintenance?"

"Jack first! Please!"

"Absolutely."

The phone rattled to the desk. In the distance, I could hear Joan talking to Manolo, the male nurse who gave the injections on Tuesdays. *Yikes.* Manolo was kind, but he was big and normally came at Jack with needles. If Jack wasn't already fleeing the building, the sight of Manolo might do the trick.

Joan came back. "Okay. Manolo and I are going to go look for him. Some of our patients here have offered to help, too. There are seven of us."

"Thank you!"

Joan and I quickly worked out a deployment plan for one person to block the main doors, while others worked backwards up the stairs, searched the main floor or swept for Jack in the parking lot. Joan's face was known and friendly; she would stand at the clinic door in case Jack returned. While she waited, she would call about the elevator.

"If you need me," I concluded ruefully, "I'll be right here."

Across the car, both radiologists were staring at me, meek and fearful, like I had left them duct taped to chairs while I robbed their offices.

Don't mess with an AutiMom!
We're bad-asses!

Posse Comitatus (Allergicus)

Through the elevator shaft, the allergy clinic search party could be heard entering the lobby and spreading out to their posts. They didn't get far.

A young voice yelled, "There he is!" This was followed by a rowdy hubbub with several people calling Jack's name, which – as you can imagine– was going to end badly.

I pressed my cheek against the doors as Jack responded with anger. "Goodbye! Goodbye," he yelled at the group. I could tell he thought he had done something wrong and that the "allergy people" were out of their usual places because of it. He was mad and embarrassed and didn't know what he was supposed to do, so he yelled "Goodbye," some more.

This spurred a scuffling of feet, and the hubbub level "went to eleven." Above the din, individual voices could be heard trying to earn Jack's trust.

"It's okay."

"Would you like some juice?"

"Calm down, buddy."

"Let's go inside and watch a video."

It was too much. Jack began screaming and, I suspect, hitting his head. I wanted to cry.

Manolo's voice boomed across the floor.

"Everybody! Back up against the wall. Look down. Look at your shoes or something — we're making him nervous. Just be ready in case he runs."

Once he had quiet, Manolo lowered his tone for Jack, "Hey, you want to hear something funny? Your mom is in the elevator, but the elevator's not going nowhere. Maybe it's out of gas?" There were some odd fart-sounding noises and an, "Oh no!"

Amazingly, Jack started to laugh.

Manolo asked, "How do you put gas in an elevator?" Squeeking sound, gulping sound, engine starter sounds. "Come oooooon, you can do it we're almost there….. Nope, it's stuck."

Jack laughed again. I could count on one hand the number of times someone other than me had made Jack laugh.

"Hey. Your mom's okay, she's just stuck. Let's go wait for her inside."

There was a verrrrrrry long stretch of silence.

Then the door to the allergy clinic opened and closed, and the lobby mob began clapping.

"Thank god." The relief made my knees wobbly. Jack would be safe, contained, and probably soon sitting down with a snack and video in the clinic's "Kiddie Corral." It no longer mattered how long we were stuck. I looked over at the radiologists cowering together in the corner. "You can scream for help now if you like."

Neither of them budged.

It was another 40 minutes before the lights came on and the elevator began moving again. As soon as the doors opened, the radiologists trampled past me to freedom.

I stopped to thank the repair man who stood off to one side, screwing a plate back onto a panel. "Did we pass our weight limit?" Yes, I asked this. I'm a horrible person.

"That would be tough. This thing is certified up to 2,000 pounds."

"What happened then?"

He shrugged. "A relay went bad. It happens. You were never in any danger."

In the "Kiddie Corral," Jack watched Tom & Jerry and enjoyed a Tootsie Pop. His upper arm now sported a small round Band-Aid. Manolo had given him his shot – probably right here, if the lingering smell of rubbing alcohol meant anything.

That's when my own mental elevator reached the top floor. *Ding!*

Before Jack could see me, I quietly backed out of the Kiddie Corral and returned to the lobby. Approaching the repairman, I asked, "When a relay goes bad, does it give off an odor?"

"An *odor?*" He laughed. "Nobody's ever asked *that* before. I mean… I suppose. But you'd have to have your nose right up against the wires to smell it." He shook his head. *People ask some crazy shit!*

When we returned for Jack's shots on Thursday, I ran a plate of fruit and cheeses up to the radiology suite. It included a note, "To my elevator co-captives," apologizing for my rude behavior. I prefer not to keep any needless enemies.

13

We Have a License for That

So! Getting back to those mysterious behaviors. I've seen them, you've seen them; they are utterly un-ignorable. But nested within them are clues to your child's unique area of intelligence. His superpower. If you asked me – and the fact that you're reading this book implies that you are seeking my opinion, harrumph – I'd say that the stranger your child behaves, the greater his intelligence is. See what I did there? I made it measureable and quantifiable; therefore: Science. Don't argue. I've even developed a handy chart showing the correlation between your child's intelligence, and your sister-in-law's reaction to his behaviors:

The Sister-In-Law
HORRORMETER

| Miffed | Concerned | Weirded Out | Totally Freaking! |

Average ◄——————— YOUR CHILD'S INTELLIGENCE LEVEL ————————► High

I'm ready to call this "Empirical Data." Thank you, thank you.

The question remains, what are these behavioral clues trying to tell us? Our kids are all different, so our answers will be different. It's up to you to decode your own kiddo. Come on! Let's go sherlocking! Put down your phone and pick up the hat.

Let me get you warmed up with two Great Tales of Discovery from my notebook.

Tale Number One:

Jack spent several years studying parked cars; I think I've mentioned that, right? Uhg! I'd be stuck rolling his sister's stroller in a circle while he walked all around these cars, having full-on flap-attacks. He'd considered every line, angle and logo. He'd stand tip toe, squat low, and even lay down at times. If any neighboring vehicles were similar, he'd move frantically between them, comparing them, part by part. He absorbed more car manufacturing secrets than were known by any non-car-industry professional on the planet, guaranteed. If competing truck makers shared the same tailgate or undercarriage or hood mold, Jack knew it.

But that's not the interesting part. Starting around the age of five, Jack would occasionally shout out a number that was not anywhere on the car he was studying. "Two hundred thirty seven," he'd shout at the Ford F150. "Eight hundred eighty four," at the Nissan 370Z.

I had a feeling he was "naming" these cars. He didn't want to confuse the yellow Jeep Renegade parked by the playground with the one in our neighbor's driveway, right? That would be rude. But how did he arrive at these Number-Names?

Yes, I lack my son's brilliance, but I am extremely tenacious. A slow, summer-long process of elimination lead me to an ingenious conclusion: Jack was adding up the license plates!

What's that? The "Alpha" part of an alphanumeric plate is un-addable? Silly girl. Jack can make math out of anything.

Say the plate said "807 RWT." Jack would read it as 868, because O-B-V-I-O-U-S-L-Y :

R is the 18th letter of the alphabet

W is the 23rd

T is the 20th

807 + 18+23+20 = 868. Don't all five year olds do this? I mean really! How could it take me all summer to figure it out?

Why would a five year old number his letters?
Duh! Because the number line makes sense and the
letter lineup doesn't.

Think about it: Does the alphabet progress according to sound?
No! Otherwise, you'd have all the vowels together, and the
consonants would be grouped according to how you form them:
Lips, roof-of-the-mouth, back-of-the-throat, etc.

Okay, well is it arranged by the complexity of each letter in
writing? No again! Otherwise L and i would come at the beginning,
and A and K would be toward the end. Shouldn't P come before B
(which is basically a P with an added bump)? Shouldn't F come
before E? And O right before Q? Why aren't W and M right next
to each other? Because, "No reason," that's why. All the letters are
just kind of thrown up on the line higgledy piggledy! Jack
numbered the letters to give them order.

Tale Number Two:

After Thanksgiving I begin meandering more as I drive around
town. Front yard Christmas decorations are one of the world's
greatest ideas: People spend their time, money and effort to light
up their homes and give total strangers a free Happiness Boost as
they drive past. The least I can do in return each year is meander.
Jack, whose shockingly accurate mental navigation system could

put Google Maps out of business, was the worst backseat driver on Earth, but he tolerated these holiday detours.

He did not, however, tolerate holiday music.

With expert arm and finger gestures, Jack would conduct his favorite children's tunes ("The bear went over the mountain, the bear went over the mountain!" "This old man, he played one! He played knick-knack on my thumb…") as Santa and Frosty floated past his window.

The December following License Plate Summer, Jack was six. His arms and legs were suddenly too long for his booster seat; in the

rearview, he looked like an octopus strapped to a sandwich. He was also no longer silent as he rode along with me; he'd begun periodically blurting out strange comments: "Seven past the five," or "Eleven past the twelve." Sometimes it seemed related to the addresses we were passing; other times I wasn't so sure. This went on all season, and it drove me half mad.

I was driving, of course, so I couldn't immediately write down the clues like I could when manning the stroller. I once tried pulling over to write a quick note, and Jack went berserk.

Never mind.

Remembering clues until we got to a stoplight was equally impossible: Everything Jack had said? Along with everything in the environment when he said it? No way! So the mystery continued to grate on me.

In January, a vital clue came home in Jack's backpack. Ooo,

worksheets from the prior semester! So scholarly! There were a few phonics exercises, primary and secondary color charts, a history packet about the Pilgrims, and, ta-da: Worksheets on telling time. Students were given digital clock illustrations and asked to draw hands on the corresponding analog clocks. The times shown on the digital clocks looked a bit like street addresses...!

What Jack had been doing on his drives with me was basically homework! He'd converted 535 Sycamore to 5:35. Little hand on the five, big hand on the seven; or as he would say it, "(Big hand) seven past the (little hand) five." Pretty clever, right? But wait, there's more!

$5:35$ = "Seven past the five"

He was also converting military time, which was *not* covered in the kindergarten worksheets: 2245 Valley Rd would become 10:45 pm and be announced by Jack as "9 past the 10".

$22:45$ = "Nine past the ten"

Or 2375 Hillside would become 11:00 pm plus 75 minutes, which of course is an additional hour and 15 minutes, making it 12:15 am in total, or "3 past the 12".

$23:75$ = "Three past the twelve"

Are you getting a headache? *Remember this is kindergarten. The kids were barely counting by fives at this point. Never mind adding, borrowing and carrying numbers with four place values while using base 10 and base 6 to the right of the colon and bases 10 and 2 on the left!*

Bear in mind, too, that as a special needs student, Jack spent most of his time in the SpEd's room (his time in class was considered both counter-productive and disruptive. It's exhausting for teachers when knuckleheaded kiddos shout "3 past the 12" for no earthly reason.) But on our drives around town, Jack sat happily adding and carrying minutes and hours on a 24 hour clock, then converting his answer to big hand/little hand terminology while conducting the children's tunes in his shrunken booster seat.

Bartender? When you have a moment?

Ahh.

Silly me, by the way. I never stopped trying to tell Jack's teachers about his extra-curricular feats of mathematics. Maybe I just did a poor job explaining it. Maybe they couldn't grasp it. Maybe it was too unbelievable. But year after year his teachers would listen in silence, mildly amused, all but patting me on the wrist.

And no joke: After a display of Jack's eerie math genius during a preschool show-and-tell, one of his first aides approached me with great enthusiasm, telling me how, after a few years of specialized training, he could someday hold down a useful job, like clearing tables at McDonalds.

Not exactly, "Anyone can grow up to become President," but, hey. Thanks for trying.

My math-oriented kiddo was understandably so bored with kindergarten arithmetic that, even with a one-on-one aide to help him at school, his grades were miserable. This was rather unhelpful to me as I tried to explain what a genius he was. I'd get daily complaints on Jack's poor cooperation, and of him sabotaging his own sessions by, for instance, shouting words for answers instead of numbers.

Wait, words? What do you mean?

An aide fetched one of Jack's worksheets from a file drawer and slapped it down in front of me. Proof of her suffering and endurance, by god. I glanced at the sheet and burst out laughing: Among the insubordinate answers were: 2 plus 3 equals "James," 6 plus 1 equals "Toby," and 4 minus 3 equals "Thomas."

14

Adventures in Potty Training

I have five books for potty training children on the Autism spectrum. Five. I can see them from where I'm sitting, tucked in the bookshelf with their pink and yellow and gold and blue and black-and-red spines, gathering dust. Each one was highly recommended by a professional in Jack's orbit. Sigh.

I want my money back. All they did was make me feel like a horrible mother – first for not diligently putting my son through their methods, and second for diligently putting my son through their methods. One of them seriously had me placing Jack on the toilet for five minutes *every thirty minutes!* Can you imagine? (Maybe you can. Maybe you have this book too. ☹) Jack thought I was punishing him and he didn't know why. It taught him to fear both the toilet and his mother, and it left him so tense that he didn't go at all until he was napping.

Toward the end of preschool, though, I was running out of runway. If Jack was still wearing a diaper when he entered kindergarten, he'd be sent home. So I read a few more articles and bought that fifth useless book and generally dragged my feet. I didn't have the guts to put Jack through another rigid method. Honestly, if I had put a dog through one of these methods, the ASPCA would have been at my door.

That got me thinking…

I grew up in southern California in a town that was still fairly rural at the time. Horses and chickens roamed many a yard, and neighbors traded eggs, grapefruit, oranges and avocados with one other. Back then, family dogs were outside animals. Our yappy mutts peppered the grass with poop and kept our neighbors up at night with their barking. Totally free spirits. But when I was seven, my best friend across the street got an exotic Springer Spaniel puppy that was going to *live in her house!* So Cocoa — that's the dog, not my friend — had to be paper trained. The seriousness with which my friend's whole family took this process made an impression on seven-year-old me.

The side door of their house led to a mud room off the kitchen. They closed all the doors to this room and covered the entire floor with overlapping sheets of newspaper. They started with 14 sheets, and for two weeks, Cocoa would stay in this room. On the second day, when they laid fresh paper down, they used 13 sheets, leaving a small square of floor exposed. The floor was new to Cocoa, so she avoided it when she pottied. The next day, they laid down 12 sheets, and the square of floor got bigger. And so it went. By the end of the two week period, there was only one sheet of newspaper in the room, and that's where Cocoa did her business. She was trained. They opened the doors and Cocoa graduated into the rest of the house. Brilliant, right? They never had to swat her, rub her nose in poop, or yell, "bad dog" at her, like other families in the neighborhood did when their dogs did a doo doo in the dining room.

And excuse me, but how were the neighborhood dogs supposed to connect these harsh punishments with their "crimes?" Even if they made the connection that "poop" = "anger," were they thinking humans didn't want them to ever have a bowel movement? Why all the random hostility?

That was the problem I had with these books! They punish the child for not understanding what the parent wants from him. Jack was nonverbal. So was Cocoa. I needed to paper train my son!

I would also need the number for a good carpet cleaner, but I'm getting ahead of my story.

Light Bulb

For decades we've been collecting and storing information that has nothing to do with autism. We've been doing this at school and work, through books, films and conversations, and from everyday life experiences. There's some good stuff in our brains! Stuff we can use for a particular situation with our particular kiddos. Trust yourself. You know more than you think you do, and nobody on earth knows your child better than you do!

Dog Days of Potty Training

Day One

Jack was five-and-three-quarters (nine-past-the-five. Ha-ha!). He was a big fan of computer games, juice boxes, and unusual sounds, so that's what I used. That first week of summer break, I turned the computer on in Jack's room and rolled the desk chair into his closet so he would have to stand. I lined up five juice boxes and a flavored water on the desk. Under the desk I laid a towel and — the magic ingredient — a large, metal bowl.

After breakfast, I dressed Jack in his favorite shirt, but only the shirt. I left him to play his computer games while I straightened up the room and cleaned his fish tank. Yeah, I was hovering, but I needed to see how things went.

The first time he peed, he was so involved in the game that he didn't much notice the "ringing" of the metal bowl. He glanced down briefly at the end, nothing more. I removed the bowl, dumped it and replaced it under the desk.

The second time the bowl began ringing, Jack looked down right away. He stopped playing to watch as the bowl filled. When he was finished, he looked at me to see if I was going to remove the bowl again for dumping. He was fast with patterns, that little man.

The third time, he looked for the bowl *before* he began peeing. That's when I knew this was going to work! I would start "removing newspapers" tomorrow.

Day Two

We had breakfast, I dressed Jack in just a shirt, and I stood him in front of the computer again. But this time I put the towel and bowl on the floor beside him to his left. He pivoted like a sprinkler head the first few times he needed the bowl, but he didn't just stand there peeing into the carpet; he sought out the bowl. Excellent.

Day Three

I placed the towel and bowl to his left again, but now it was two steps away from where he stood. My fear at this point was that he'd pull the bowl closer to his desk for convenience, but he didn't. I think it's because the bowl was parked on the towel. The towel created a kind of "bowl station" that Jack saw as fixed in place, even though the station itself was moving from one day to the next. But consider what he now taught himself to do without any direction, coercion or punishment:

- ☑ Recognize the need to pee.
- ☑ Stop what he was doing to address it.
- ☑ Walk to a specific place to do it.

This crazy method was working!

Day Four

I placed the towel and bowl four steps away from him, and just outside his bathroom door.

Today the bowl was moved to the other side of the bathroom door. The threshold might have caused Jack to stop and view the "bathroom bowl" as something different than the "bedroom bowl," so I turned the towel lengthwise and let about six inches of it extend invitingly into the bedroom. Bingo.

Day Six

The towel and bowl were placed on the floor directly in front of the toilet.

Day Seven

Today the bowl was placed on top of the toilet seat. The towel was no longer being used, but I didn't want it to be suddenly gone since I was already throwing Jack a curve with the change in the bowl's level. I dropped the towel down between the toilet and the wall where he could easily see it, but where it seemed "out of commission." The experiment went off without a hitch.

Day Eight

Drum roll please! I removed the towel and turned the bowl sideways so it could fit down in that same space between the wall and the toilet. The bowl was now "out of commission." Jack walked in to find it, and as he stood there wondering if he should pick it up, he began peeing into the toilet. It was a deeper sound than what he got from the bowl and it caught his attention immediately. He was hooked.

Last Days

I left him pant-less for another day. On Day Ten I dressed him in loose underwear. On Day Twelve, I added pull-on shorts. And that was it! No tears, no tantrums and no emotional scars — for either of us.

Who's a good boy!

15

Choices

So we were heading out of Safeway at maybe 9:00pm; not late by our home's standards, but dark and well past prime shopping hours. The smaller stores along the strip mall had already closed, so there weren't many customers milling around. In the parking lot's traffic lane beside us, the occasional car zipped by unimpeded.

I had a loaded cart with a two-year old in the seat, and I had Jack. He was six, non-verbal, and seriously fascinated by cars: He could stand in one place for 10 minutes having a total flap attack as he stared at the back of a parked vehicle. And yes, he was likely to do this in a parking lot. Even if it was night. Even if it was a snowy night in February.

I put both his hands on the cart handle and walked behind him as he "help me" push the cart down the slushy, sloping sidewalk. I had parked the car about 50 yards ahead, close to where the sidewalk sloped down to the traffic lane. But Jack spotted a flap-worthy pickup truck nearby. Before I knew it, he had ducked out from under my arms and bolted into the traffic lane.

Now I had a choice: Abandon my two-year old, my purse and about $200 in groceries to chase Jack, or hang onto the cart and scream out after a boy I knew wouldn't respond to the sound of his own name.

"Jack!"

Skid.

Honk!

"Mommeeeee!"

By the time I had Jack by the elbow, the cart his sister was in had rolled down the slope, hit a patch of slush, turned sideways, and begun to tip over. Had I made the right decision? Seconds ago, Jack was in real danger. But the car didn't hit him, and the fall his sister was about to take looked life-altering. It's one of those intense, heart-stopping moments that still wakes me up at night.

I know you've had one of these. Maybe more than one. Chances are we'll both go through others. I just wanted to tell you that I understand. When you're forced to make split-second decisions, weighing all the likely outcomes and choosing primly from among them simply isn't possible. You have to act right now. Sometimes something bad will happen as a result of that split-second choice. I urge you not to blame yourself. The worst thing you could ever do is make no choice at all.

Let me refill your drink.

My story here turned out well, thank god, knock wood. There are some incredible people living in my town, and three of them happened to appear right there when my daughter needed them most. I'm so grateful they realized what was happening fast enough to take action. The driver who had honked at Jack jumped out of his car to race after my daughter. A couple leaving Dominos got to the cart first, dropping their pizza in the process. The woman pulled my falling two-year-old into her arms.

I should have replaced the pizza. I should have sent them all flowers and written them Christmas cards for the rest of my life. But I was O.D.ed on adrenalin and didn't even think to ask their names. Honestly, I can't remember loading the car or driving home. Everything is a blank. Since then, I've probably walked passed these good Samaritans several times without knowing it.

If any of them, by the remotest chance, happens to be reading this book, let me say how sorry I am that I didn't give you the appreciation you deserved right then on that February night. Thank you for being there for my family when we needed you. The difference you made for my daughter was — at a minimum — monumental. You will forever be our heroes.

Thumbs Up For Handicap Parking!

If your autistic kiddo is a parking lot flight-risk, most states will grant you a handicap placard. I got one for Jack shortly after our parking lot nightmare. Fewer steps mean fewer chances of disaster. The placard has also been great on those snowy mornings when I could pull right up to the school's front door like a limo! An awesome perk, girlfriend, and a real no-brainer. Drop everything and go Google your state's application right now!

16

Let's All Coexist!

People love to use the butt of their cars to inform us about their hobbies, pets, children, political viewpoints and miscellaneous other obsessions while we patiently wait for them to notice the light has turned green. It makes them happy, but honestly. Why should we bother learning about strangers who are locked away in a metal box? We'll probably never meet them, so why groom us with this knowledge? Are they hoping we'll pull up beside them, roll down our windows and say, "Excuse me, but could you tell me a little bit more about why we should 'Get the hell out of the Middle East?'"

My take on it is: Communication should have a shared purpose. A bumper sticker that says, "Student Driver at the Wheel" is useful to me. It changes the way I interact with your car. I'll be more patient. I won't get irked if your turn signal stays on for 6 blocks. I'll give you a wide berth as I pass. These small courtesies I extend to you will in turn make it easier for you to practice driving. See? Shared purpose. Whereas our driving relationship isn't improved by me learning you heart your yorkie.

One snowy Saturday when Jack was 6, I took him to Chuck E. Cheese's. The place was jammed. I never sat down or played a game with his sister, but I still had a hard time keeping Jack in my sights. The crowds kept cutting us off and pushing him beyond my reach. Separated farther and farther from Jack, I watched helplessly as one kid stole a string of tickets from him. Another walked away with his token cup – that looked like an accident, but it didn't matter since I couldn't get to him to stop it. More importantly, I saw several parents yell at Jack – really get into his face, pointing, gesturing, and ganging up against him with their kids. I saw them push Jack back, pull him aside by the arm, and edge him out at games. In response, I went foam-at-the-mouth rabid on some of these parents, which probably scared Jack as much as the initial confrontations.

Light Bulb!

Jack needed a
"Student Driver" bumper sticker.

As bad as these parents had been with Jack, I didn't believe they were flat-out cruel. If they'd known Jack was disabled, I was sure they'd have treated him differently.

On the way home we stopped at Target where I bought a white T-shirt and a package of iron-on printer paper. The shirt I created carried a bold, big-lettered message on both the front and the back.

It said:

> # I'm Autistic
> ## and functionally
> ## Non-Verbal.
> ## If you need help,
> ## ask for
> ## Jack's Mom.

Below that, I put my cell phone number, in case he got away from me in a large or crowded place. I used no distracting clip art, no fancy fonts and only two colors. This was not fashion. It was a billboard.

If there was one thing I did above all else
to help my son, this was it.

The world utterly changed for Jack. No longer did strangers randomly swoop in to scream at him. People saw the shirt before they even saw Jack's face, and this let them be ready for whatever interaction was coming. Jack was given space, deference, and the benefit of the doubt, so he could move through a crowd with confidence. People stopped staring or laughing whenever he did something odd, and they stopped complaining when he took too long. Instead, they would sidle up to me and quietly rave about his shirt.

And I'll tell you! Before the shirt, whenever someone who had been hassling or lecturing Jack found out that he was disabled, they were universally mortified.

U-N-I-V-E-R-S-A-L-L-Y M-O-R-T-I-F-I-E-D !!!

It ruined their day every bit as much as it ruined Jack's. Nobody wants to be the bad guy in our stories. Okay, *some people do*, but nobody within a reasonable margin of psychological balance wants that on their conscience. A bumper-sticker T-shirt gives strangers the chance to be the good guys they want to be. Cheers!

Weird Autism Myth #3

Children With Autism Prefer Social Isolation

Some kids with autism think so quickly, and with such intensity, that interacting with mere mortals is a letdown. So for them, yeah; maybe they aren't terribly keen to connect with that chubbo across the room who is busy sticking a crayon up his nose. Mom says, "Why don't you go play?" Her kid's like, "With *that* guy?! You must be joking!"

Just because your child may not speak doesn't mean he doesn't have standards!

Jack, on the other hand, probably would have found Crayon Kid fascinating. I expect he would have stood two feet away, staring and stimming, squealing with joy, as he watched that crayon disappear into the kid's nostril. Mind you, this isn't a sign of peer bonding. If Crayon Kid had turned to Jack, offered him a stick and said, "Here! You try," Jack would have smacked it away and retreated with an angry bellow. He wasn't big on interaction, but he was hugely drawn to other kids. He loved to see them talk, play, climb, laugh,

> "Hey Mom! That guy seems nice... No, that toothless meth-head on the corner begging for money. Why don't you go play with him?"

fight, fall down, cry, sneeze, poke straws into juice boxes, and sneak off to poop under the slide. Even though he wasn't ready to play with others, nobody in their right mind would have concluded that Jack "preferred social isolation."

I have to tell you, though – the treatment our kids sometime get from their peers give them every reason to punch the "social eject button." So far, Jack hasn't done that but... *Yikes.* I'm knocking wood.

17

¡Apártate!

So, how does a non-verbal, socially-seeking kid navigate the peer-world? He develops a super-duper, yo-mama, honkin'-long social antenna. He learns to recognize gait, carriage, group flocking patterns, verbal tones, hand gestures, body language, facial expression, and every combination thereof. *Zum beispiel*:

A kid with his hands on his head:

...who is sitting alone, had a fight with someone and may be crying.

... and is running, is hurt and needs help in a hurry.

... and is loping along beside her friends, is about to laugh.

... who stops suddenly, realizes he left something very important behind.

Jack's field of vision wrapped around him in a near 360° circle. He could stand in one place staring into the middle distance—squinting and finger flicking — taking it all in at once. Sure, some kids may give him a weird look as they walk by, or glance at their friends before giggling. No biggie. Jack took that in, too, as part of the massive school-recess-data-sweep. He knew where everyone was, where they were headed, what they were doing, and how they felt about it... he had more data than the CIA!

Long before Jack could speak, he had mastered the language of non-verbal social cues. **You cannot fool our kids, girlfriend.**

114

Body language doesn't lie.

Back then, Jack had a severe feeding disorder, too. He was probably the only kid at his school who dreaded lunchtime. To help buck him up as he stared into his lunchbox, I'd taken to slipping in toys, pictures, jokes and various other surprises. His classmates quickly caught on and were soon gathered around Jack each day as he unzipped his lunch.

Yes! The school <u>did</u> complain about this, thank you for asking! We were told it was disruptive and unfair to allow Jack to have personal items at the lunch table when the other children were denied this right. So Jack's doctor wrote a note claiming therapeutic need. Boom! We love you, Dr. Z!

You know how it is: Everything I did for Jack was an experiment. Some things worked, others didn't, and he couldn't tell me which was which. Every three to six weeks I booked time with the school to follow Jack around for the day, watching, taking notes, and making adjustments to my "Jacksperiments."

During one such visit, a tiny transforming car in Jack's lunchbox drew a tight crowd of admirers at lunch. Jack didn't know how to manipulate it, but he was more interested in watching his classmates as they fiddled with it, argued over it and passed it from hand to hand. The boy next to Jack, reaching out for his turn, found the hubbub of kids inching farther away. He sat back down, unwrapped his sandwich and place it on top of his lunch bag. He looked in Jack's lunchbox and asked him, "What are you having for lunch, Jack?"

The question pulled Jack away from his study of kids wrestling with the toy. He didn't know what the boy had asked him, but he recognized that he'd been called to focus on something specific. He saw the sandwich sitting on top of the lunch bag. Was that it? He reached over and touched the top of the sandwich.

The kid with the sandwich said, "That's my lunch. I'm having a turkey sandwich. What are you having, Jack?"

Jack went ballistic.

He screamed wordlessly at Sandwich Kid. He got up from the table and screamed again. He paced back and forth, crying and flapping, then he stopped and screamed at the back of the boy's head.

Sandwich Kid ducked and covered head with his arms. He had no idea what was happening or why – he'd been trying to be nice. Isn't that what you're supposed to do?

The classmates fighting over the transforming car looked at Jack with alarm. A teacher began walking their way. The last kid holding the car slipped it back into Jack's lunchbox, and the group hustled back to their seats here and there along the table. Seeing this, Jack cried harder. He plucked the car out of his lunchbox and threw it to the ground where it broke into several pieces.

All this happened in the short time it took me to get up and circle around to Jack's side of the table. "Hey, it's okay. Let's go sit outside." I zipped up his lunchbox and handed it to him. "You want to?" Jack calmed down enough to see that I was pointing to an empty table outside under a tree. He started for the door.

Before following, I plucked up the car pieces and apologized to the kids at the table loud enough for the teacher to hear. "I'm sorry," I told them. "You guys are great classmates. I don't know what happened." But I did know. It was glaringly obvious…

116

Sandwich Kid's Words	Sandwich Kid's Body Language	Jack's Experience
		Jack is enjoying the tussle over the toy car. Some kids are more aggressive and seem to know what to do, others want to try even though they're not that familiar with transforming toys, others still are there to be part of the action; shouting and reaching without taking the toy.
	Sandwich Kid Jack stops reaching for the car and sits down. He is getting his lunch out.	Sandwich Kid is less aggressive. He will wait for his turn to play with the car. Meanwhile, he isn't interested in watching the other kids play.
"What are you having for lunch, Jack?"	He wants Jack's attention. He wants Jack to look at their lunches. He's gesturing at his sandwich.	Sandwich Kid asks for Jack's attention. Jack would rather watch the kids playing with his car, but he recognizes a kind tone and decides to comply. Sandwich Kid wants Jack to see his sandwich. Why? Is it similar to Jack's? Is Jack supposed to compare them? Jack reaches for the kid's sandwich.
"That's my lunch. I'm having a turkey sandwich. What are you having, Jack?"	Sandwich Kid pulls his sandwich away from Jack's outreached hand. Sandwich Kid's eyes have widened and his smile is mildly stretched out of shape. He looks nervous and a little upset.	No, Jack did the wrong thing! Sandwich kid thinks Jack is bad, and he's upset that Jack touched his food! He isn't a friend! He tricked Jack into doing something wrong. Everyone's looking! Jack had been happy until Sandwich Kid tricked him, and now people are upset with Jack because Jack is angry that Sandwich Kid tricked him. It isn't fair. Sandwich Kid was to blame. Now the other kids no longer want to play with Jack's car because Jack can't stop yelling. Everything's ruined. Everything is ruined because of Sandwich Kid.

Sandwich Kid had been reaching out to Jack in kindness. Jack, however, didn't understand his outreach because it was verbal. Jack couldn't "hear" him, but he *could* read Sandwich Kid's body language, which, in its clumsiness, communicated something very different than his words.

There was no fixing this today. Right now my job was to calm Jack. We sat alone at the table under the tree playing with the reassembled car. I rolled the car up to a ladybug on the table, screeched it to a halt, transformed it into a robot and had it run away from the bug in terror. Then I did it again. And again. And again. Jack laughed and ate his lunch. By the time class resumed, he was fine.

Later, I wrote a note to staff in hopes they would put Jack and Sandwich Kid together in another situation so their relationship could be refreshed. I don't know if they ever did. But I never saw the two of them side by side at lunch again.

On the bright side, non-verbal kids don't care what language you speak. I've released Jack into play groups speaking Korean, Spanish and Hindi. The mannerisms were different with each group – (I think of them as "physical dialects") – but Jack had no trouble getting the rhythms of their play.

He especially enjoyed watching the town's Hispanic kids at the large park down by the lake. They were loud, vibrant and very expressive. When going down the slide, they didn't just wave and say, "Mom! Watch me!" They said, "Mom! Look how high I am! I'm going to go faster than a car! Are you watching? Are you ready? Do you see how far down that is? I'll be going so fast that I'll be like a bullet. Are you ready? Aunt Alma! You watch too! This will be incredible!"

Their body language was big and vivid: They doubled-over when they laughed. They ran away screaming when they were scared, then they would turn back and complain loudly about whatever had scared them – gesturing and readdressing the issue for five minutes. When they got mad, they pushed each other, with victims falling to the ground or crashing backwards into third parties. Sides would form – older kids vs younger kids; girls against boys – yelling, pushing, storming off and returning, then a truce would be struck and the laughter would return. Jack was riveted.

Another thing he probably liked about these kids was the sheer size of their play groups. At the park near our house, Jack might stumble across two or three kids playing, and when he stopped to watch them, his presence was as subtle as Clifford the Dog. How could they not notice him? Once he was noticed, he was invariably invited to join in… which would cause him to yell and run away. But here at the lake, twelve to twenty kids could be playing together. Even if they noticed Jack, no individual kid felt it was his job to invite Jack into the game; someone else could do it, and as far as each kid was concerned, someone else probably already had. This freed Jack to wander through the group and get a good view of all their interactions without worry. Once in a while a child would shout something like, "Hey! Is this blonde kid on our team?" But that was it.

The year his sister was born, Jack spent from spring through fall insistently gesturing each turn the car should make in order to bring us to this park. I would then sit in the shade with his newborn sister, brushing up on Spanish and absorbing the Chihuahuense dialect. It was delightful.

And then it came to an end.

That day, one of the girls was lying sideways in the sand at the bottom of the long slide. The other kids took turns sliding down fast enough to fly over this girl before hitting the sand. Some of the older kids slid head-first on their bellies and dove over her into a somersault. The younger ones slowed to a stop and stepped off the slide onto her back. Everyone laughed. Everyone squealed. Everyone wanted to go again.

Jack was not quite four that day, and he had never climbed a play structure without my "spotting" him. When I saw him mount the main platform and head for the stairs to the tall slide on the second level tower, I was thrilled/shocked/proud/terrified — an emotional combo-punch that may be unique to AutiMoms. I tucked my daughter into the baby carriage and pushed it little closer to the structure to watch. Was he ready for this?

Jack was following a boy who looked six or seven. Reaching the top of the tower stairs, Slide Boy yelled through the guardrails to the mothers, aunts and adult cousins at a picnic table. "Hey! Watch me! I'm going to go on my stomach! I'm doing a stomach slide this time! I'm going to fly like Superman and go right over Camila. Like Superman! I'm going right now!"

Slide Boy's enthusiasm emboldened Jack. He climbed up the stairs to the tower without hesitation, and as Slide Boy sat down on the slide, Jack took the last stair, placing him right behind Slide Boy. He bent down over Slide Boy's shoulder to get a slider's-eye view down the chute.

Just then, Slide Boy realized he wasn't on his stomach. He started to get up and found Jack right on top of him. "Oye, tú," he yelled at Jack. "¡Apártate!" He then shoved Jack off the stairs.

"Oh my god!"

Jack did a ¾ cartwheel in the air and hit the main platform hard on his side. He sat up and looked around, disoriented and scared. Behind him was an opening in the guardrail for access to a fireman's pole, and I knew what was about to happen. I let go of the baby carriage and rushed forward as Jack looked around to find me. As he turned, he fell right through the opening and down another five feet to the sand.

"Jack!"

Before I could reach him, Jack was already on his feet – which was a relief; he wasn't badly injured. But he screamed with such fury that it scared me out of my wits. Everyone around the play structure – kids and adults – stopped what they were doing to look at him.

And there it was again, poor Jack: He had been gravely assaulted by Slide Boy, but everyone was staring at *him*, which to Jack meant *he* was the one who had done something wrong.

Jack ran right past me, out of the sand, and up the grass slope to our car parked just above. There he continued to scream and slap the door to the back seat.

Kids began leaping down from the play structure in every direction. They ran past me to the picnic table where their mothers sat. Slide Boy went down the slide on his fanny and ran over to join them. I pointed at him and yelled, "Whose child is this?! Which one of you is his mother?! Did you see what he did?!"

Most of them already knew I spoke Spanish; we'd be sharing casual pleasantries for weeks. Still, the women seemed surprised that I could use it in anger. They couldn't pretend not to understand me, so they looked at one another and spoke quietly. When the whispering ended, they shrugged and swiped leisurely at their cellphones, avoiding my eye contact. The kids, still gathering into a deep group behind them, began smiling and giggling.

"This isn't funny," I scolded them. "My son could have been killed!"

Something fell into the sand behind me as three more kids ran past to join the others.

I turned to find the baby carriage tipped over. My daughter started to scream.

"Oh my sweet love!" I picked her up into my arms and

straightened the carriage. "Did you kids do that on purpose?!" I looked over at the group. They were all laughing now. Even the mothers.

Jack continued crying and slapping the car door.

I won't bother telling you what I said to that big family as I left the sand, but I lived in Spain for years and learned how to curse rather well. I let it fly. Not that it made any difference. They continued laughing as I:

- ☑ Pushed the carriage up to the parking lot
- ☑ Opened the car
- ☑ Removed the carrier from the carriage
- ☑ Belted my daughter's into the car
- ☑ Helped my son into his car seat
- ☑ Checked him for injuries
- ☑ Belted him in
- ☑ Folded the carriage
- ☑ Stowed it in cargo area
- ☑ Closed the back of the car and
- ☑ Got into the driver's seat

A couple of them waved sarcastically, perhaps knowing we would never be back, which turned out to be true. As we pulled away, Jack dug into the "completion phrase" his ABA therapist used: "All done. All done. All done with the park. All done."

It's been almost a decade now. But whenever I think of this incident I still curse in Spanish.

18

Absolutely Animated

Our bookcase covers an entire wall and is packed with hefty tomes. But our collection of children's videos outnumbers our books two to one. There's no bookcase to quarantine these, so they've swarmed the house and nested at will. You'll find them lined up, stacked up, bursting out of shoeboxes, tossed under beds, and stuffed into drawers and between couch cushions. My children won't let me donate a single one – not even a Baby Einstein! So I've chosen not to see them anymore; not as the vacuum cleaner sets off a domino line, nor as the dust rag sends another one clattering down behind a dresser. If you stop by, be careful where you step.

By the age of four, Jack had mastered the remote for the DVD player, and was play/pausing these movies to enjoy them with microscopic scrutiny. Play...pause, squeal, was his routine. One frame at a time. He'd bulls-eye in on that moment between a twist in the plot and a character's reaction to it: Yosemite Sam's face goes from confident to confused, then his eyes grow bigger and his head tilts back and his mouth starts to open and his mustache straightens as it's dragged through the air and his eyebrows arch upward. All so fascinating! His next line, "Run for your lives," didn't interest Jack. He'd rewind back to Bugs' knowing look as the shaking ground announces the coming stampede, then he'd play-pause-squeal his way through it again.

It cracked me right up, when it wasn't driving me crazy.

Visitors would develop facial tics and demand to know why he couldn't just let the video play. "I don't know," was my stock answer, but I do have a theory: There's an emotional and psychological evolution happening in the transition zone between words, and for nonverbal kids, this is where the story is. It speaks directly to them in a way that is deeply satisfying. Take a fresh look at your cartoons. There's real blue-ribbon artwork poured into these transitions. I'd gone my whole life without giving them a thought. Now it's another chalk mark on the Big Board of Stuff I Learned from Jack.

Don't give me that look! That, "Well, duh. My kid likes videos too. What's your point," look. Put down your margarita while I quickly slap you upside the head.

Use it! Use it, use it, *use it!* If your house is overrun with something — movies, stuffed animals, Legos — your child has sent you a signal! Use it!! This is such a globally-important point that it deserves its own call-out:

Use It!!!

When you see your child enjoying something, use it!! He has shown you a rare — perhaps fleeting — window into his mind! Use it to get your child from where *he* wants to be to where *you want him* to be. You are a mother, and nature in her wisdom has granted you an extra scoop of deviousness! So when you see your child enjoying something it is your JOB to find a way to use it to advance toward your selfish maternal goals!

I need a compact travel soapbox that I can pull from my purse and pop open for use anytime, anywhere, then quickly fold and return to my purse. Product developers at Telebrands, take note.

Jack liked cartoons, so I made "live action cartoons" for him starring Mom. Mom's Cell Phone Productions. All kinds of moments in Jack's everyday life made worthy plots for my cartoons. For example:

Door opens to Jack's bedroom. Camera pans left and right, looking around. It then stops abruptly as it discovers a shirt on the floor. Camera zooms in and out as we hear mom say, "Is that... DIRTY LAUNDRY?!" Camera pans to Mom's horrified face, back to shirt, back to Mom's horrified face, back to shirt. Mom's foot enters shot as she gingerly tries to step over shirt. Much visual confusion as Mom falls violently to the floor. Camera settles on Mom's face as she lies on the ground, fighting off death. She pulls shirt into view. Using her forearm, she drags herself across the room to the hamper. We see the arm reach weakly up, struggling to get the shirt into the hamper as Mom can be heard rasping, "Laundry basket..." With the shirt safely in the hamper, Mom dies.

Oh yeah! My Mom Movies are loud, overdramatic and pitched right at Jack's funny bone. But they're not pointless. Here, Jack learned the phrases "dirty laundry" and "laundry basket," and he developed a generalized understanding of their meaning. He also never left dirty clothes on his floor again — not because he was afraid of being punished, but because he now knew what people do with their dirty laundry. I made dozens of these videos, and kept several of them on my phone at any time for Jack to enjoy while we were waiting at the doctor's or therapist's office, sitting in traffic, or whenever we were idle for more than a few minutes. Jack played them and replayed them, honoring my artistry with his signature squeal.

And The Award Goes To...

Jack and Company wishes to salute the animation artists who bother to craft the detailed transitional frames that deliver story to the nonverbal community. To this end, we are establishing the first ever GASP! Awards.

- The First Place GASP! goes to Pixar Animation, whose contributions include developing an estimated 120 frames of emotional-reaction-at-a-time into the faces of toys and motor vehicles.

- In Second Place is Classic Loony Toons, and the ground breaking artists who led the way for an entire industry. Gentlemen, after nearly 90 years, your work still delights.

- The Third Place GASP! goes to Disney Animation whose transitions tend to be rich and dense with more complex emotion. Many of our kids don't grow into these films until their mid-teens, but when they do, these cartoons are socially nourishing.

- The Honorable Mentions goes to Sony Animation. While the more frantic pace of Sony cartoons leaves less space for transitions, the artists manage to cram a lot of story into them.

Additional rulings by the Judges:

- The facial features of Charlie Brown characters are too small and stylized to communicate emotion without help from the dialog. Therefore, the GASP Awards Committee sadly disqualifies the Peanuts series from competing.

- Japanese anime skips transitional frames. Characters jump from maybe 30 frames of static calm to a complete change of expression. "Now I am surprised," they say. Two thumbs down!

19

Can You Hear Me Now?

In my twenties — my Pre-pre-AutiMom Era, if you will — I worked in international advertising. While overseas, I learned a hearty slab of Japanese and German, a dollop of Italian, a sliver of French, a pinch of Swedish, and a five-course meal's-worth of Spanish (with a coffee and cognac to finish). But most of my European friends thought this accomplishment was *adorable*, because *they* were outright *fluent* in *four or more languages!* Seriously. When inviting me to the movies, they never bothered to mention what language the film was in, because to them it didn't matter. We'd end up watching, say, a Greek film with French subtitles, and I'd spend the whole movie pestering them to explain why they were laughing. The thing is, they started learning their second and third languages at the age of zero, which gave them a full 20+-year jump on me. "This will not happen to any child of mine," I determined. "No way!"

And so, ten years before having kids, I decided I would speak to those future kids in multiple languages from day one. Get them in the crib, before they're old enough to escape on hands and knees.

Poor Jack. He was my test-case baby.

When he hadn't begun early verbal interaction by 13 months, I wasn't concerned. After all, he was busy digesting much more language than the neighbor's kids. My family squawked that I was confusing him, and in hindsight my experiment couldn't have been helpful. At the time, though, I poo-pooed their pedestrian blather. I had a plan and my child was superior and I knew that someday they would be humbled before his brilliance.

When he passed the 18 month mark with no progress, I cut out everything but English and Spanish.

By 22 months I was pushing Tarzan-speak. All hopes of having a designer child had evaporated. But you know what? The not-a-designer-child let-down happens to *all* first time parents, not just us. So no worries.

But, of course, I *was* worried. Even his doctor was no longer telling me to, "Just wait and see." This is when the word "audiologist" first knocked on my door, and for the next year, it all but moved in with us.

Jack's hearing wasn't just good, it was *spooky good!* He recognized the specific engine and driving rhythms of his dad's car coming home when it was still blocks away. Who else but a dog can do that? And he could tell when his favorite bag of chips was rustling open in the hands of a poacher *on another floor, even with TV, stereo and video games playing!* Did you know different chip bags make different sounds? Apparently they do! Never once has Jack race down after a Dorito-Rustler only to catch the varmint red-handed with a bag of Ruffles. Shamefully, there's no place on a medical form to put this crucial, diagnostic insight. And so for the better part of a year, nearly every new medical pro that looked at Jack requested his or her very own hearing test.

Flash Rant

Hearing Test Horrors!

I'm talking to *you*, Doctor or Therapist du jour insisting I have Jack's hearing checked for the gazillionth time. What a waste of Jack's patience; making him lie around while probes are stuffed into his ear canals! Clamping giant headphones down on his head and running screech-tones through the wire. Or sitting him in a dark room to see how he responds to toys randomly jumping to life, beating drums and crashing cymbals together. Total Nightmare Mix! How's *your* hearing, Doc? Is my son crying loud enough for ya?!

I'm betting they all own stock in the audiology clinic. (Haughty sniff.)

Meanwhile, I was busy cramming language into my son. Part of this effort involved buying any toy that spoke, from books, maps and an electronic dictionary, to various animatronic plush characters and a wearable brain on a spring. Even Jack's favorite trainset set spoke, and that one, my friend, warrants its own chapter!

At the peak of this purchasing frenzy, we had at least 200 talking toys. I couldn't tidy Jack's room without a dozen of them giving me sass. The average cost of each item was $67, not including the requisite truckload of batteries. Do the math. I've already done it, but have pity on me; the answer is too depressing to type. I call it an "investment," then look away and move on.

But it prompts me to ask: Do *you* still have a retirement account? If not, do not be ashamed. I've got an AutiMom motto that a lot of us might as well frame and hang in our front halls:

Foolish is he who saves for a rainy day while a typhoon is parked on his roof.

I guess the real question is, did these talking toys help Jack? The jury is still out. They did help him understand that sentences aren't simply the human-equivalent of barking; that they transmit complex ideas from one person to another. But the sentences these toys spoke sounded exactly the same each time they were spoken; the music, rhythm, pace and tone of the sentences never varied. To Jack, these were sound streams[3] conveying a unique message. Jack never heard the independent, interchangeable words sitting within a given sound stream. This is why I'm not sure the toys were helpful. They may, in fact, have delayed Jack's speech even further.

For example, Jack's animatronic skiing Tigger said, "Look out belooooooowwww," as he skied, flipped and rolled along. Listen to that in your head: The first two words were short and high, and the last word stretched downward across half an octave. Jack, of course, memorized that sentence immediately. But if I said to him, "***Look*** at this picture," or "Let's get ***out*** the bath toys," or "It's on the shelf ***below***," he wouldn't recognize these same three words because they weren't nested in skiing Tigger's sound stream.

Once, as an experiment, I used the "music" of skiing Tigger's sound stream with replacement words: "Get out the blooooooooocks," Again, listen to that in your head and consider its

---

[3] I hope you like the expression "sound stream," because I made it up, and I'm about to use it a lot!

similar sound. Jack was maybe 20 feet away in the dining room when I tested this sentence. He looked up with a bright expression on his face and walked over to join me. Then his smile dropped. He expected to find me like Tigger, skiing and flipping across the kitchen floor. Instead, I was holding a lame-o box of blocks. He turned and walked out, leaving Mom totally egg-faced.

That's when I developed Jack's Mom's Cockamamie Theory, or JMCT for short. You will not be the first to mock me, should you so choose, but the JMCT was solid enough for me to work with, and that's all I cared about.

This Is My Brain. This Is My Brain Is On A Spring. Any Questions?

My JMCT is based on the heightened sensory perception and jaw-dropping memories that many spectrum children exhibit. With that kind of mental power at their disposal, I believe many of them see the memorization of entire sentences — including tone and inflection — as a reasonable expectation. So they buckle down to do a job that could take decades, even for them. Consider this: The average English speaker has a vocabulary of about 5,000 words. That means a neurotypical child, over the course of childhood and adolescence, memorizes 5,000 unique, thought-transmitting sounds. That's a totally doable task, as you and I both serve to prove.

But!

These words combine to make *millions of sentences*, with different shades of meaning and social hierarchy. Add variations in mood, tone and inflection and you're looking at maybe *10s of millions* of sentences that our kiddos may be trying to memorize as unique, thought-transmitting sound streams, one by one. I'm exhausted just thinking about it!

If medical professionals are using the word "echolalia" to describe your child's use of language, I personally believe you have a child with some serious horsepower.

Let's pause a moment, grab a goat and a cup of hot cocoa, and take quick tour of echolalia.

(Oh. Ha-ha-ha. That wasn't the cocoa.)

20

Repeat After Me

So no, it's not an Alpine town or yodeling game. Echolalia is a fancy term for a phase that all kids pass through where they "echo" what's said to them. You say "bye-bye" to an 11 month old, and she says "bye-bye" back, but if you don't then leave, she won't call you out: "Hey lady! I thought you were going bye bye!"

As language abilities grow, true replies start replacing the echo. By the age of three, echolalia is typically in the dumpster.

But what our kids are doing is a little more sophisticated. Therapists call it "delayed echolalia," and by this they don't mean the echolalia stage starts later than usual (although that is often the case). What they mean is, the child is not echoing a statement he just heard. Instead, he heard it a while ago – maybe *months* ago – and it's been stored ever since in mental Tupperware. The memory stays fresh and out of the way until something in the child's environment pops the Tupperware seal. It's typically a sensory input that's too small for a busy parent to even notice, like a draft in the room, the movement of a shadow, the smell of laundry soap, or the buzzzzz-bump of a fly hitting a window. These small, sensory inputs get tangled up with the statement at the time the child first hears it. So when that small, sensory input reoccurs, the child pulls the matching statement out of storage and begins to recite.

And we're not talking "bye-bye" anymore. We may be talking the entire soundtrack of Zootopia. As you know, our kids can really get on a roll with these things and will often go bananas if you try to interrupt them — which can be a real drag when you're already late for the dentist.

Sometimes they'll get part-way through and go back to the beginning again. (Aaack!!)

Sometimes they'll get into a loop where they'll repeat some middle passage again and again before continuing on. (Errgh!!)

Maybe they'll get all the way to the end, or maybe they'll just stop for reasons unknown. (Phew!)

But the lid then goes back on the Tupperware and the memory is tucked away for another time. Unless it becomes one of their favorites. Then they may leave it on the counter to enjoy obsessively for a while. (Oh goody....)

I know it drives you bonkers, but here's the thing: Our kids are doing something A*M*A*Z*I*N*G! They are lasering in on a memory and recreating it sound by sound! You and I couldn't do this if the NSA begged us and offered us a billion dollars in order to help save all of humanity! Our kids do this because they *can*, it's *interesting*, and it's probably the most fun they've had all day.

Of course we push for social interaction with our kids, and I've got some tips on that which I'll get to shortly. But it doesn't have to be a 24/7 slog. Relax. I say go ahead and let your kiddo enjoy his natural center of balance, and the grooming of a talent that is almost unearthly. Who cares if your sister in law gets a frowny-face? Isn't that kind of a bonus? And come on: If our five year olds were already breaking Olympic track and field records, would we duct tape them to a chair to keep them from knocking over the lamp? No! We'd move the lamp!

Who needs a medical degree when you're this brilliant?

Oh! Then there's this: You know how people say you shouldn't wake up a sleepwalker (which may not even be true, but people still say it and most people aren't willing to take any chances, including me as you will see in a later chapter)? A delayed echolalia episode may fall into the same bucket. These memories can be so intense that our kids are almost time-travelling. If they could answer us, I bet they could tell us which toys were precisely where in the room during the moment of that memory, and if an airplane or motorcycle could be heard anywhere in the distance, whether a juice box was left on the table, what flavor it was, and if that table needed dusting. I believe they could tell us what they were wearing, if they had an "owie" somewhere on their body that was healing, and what the neighbor next door was cooking. Our kids are fully in that moment, and whatever they're saying is simply that moment's soundtrack. Ripping our kids out of these moments may not necessarily be dangerous, but it's gotta rank somewhere between inconsiderate and cruel.

Hopefully it doesn't rank with sleep deprivation, because life is going on, here. Right? Sometimes the school bus is waiting, it's starting to hail, or a lawn mower is headed right at us, so we have to jolt our kids back into the moment. But when stopping them isn't required, it may be healthier to leave them be. I say "may," because I'm not a neurologist or psychologist. But there's a reason our kids feel compelled to do this, and I'm not sure anyone fully understands what that is.

Flash Back, Baby!

When Jack was four, a friend stopped by with her three year old daughter in tow. This young girl tried to get Jack to help her build a tower with blocks, but that wasn't his thing. He sat on a footstool and watched as she built the tower without him; the blocks going higher and higher. Eventually the tower tipped over. "Kuh-ther-bah-thumped" was the sound it made as it hit the carpet, while a few stray pieces clattered sharply across the coffee table. That perfect combination of sounds popped the Tupperware seal on one of Jack's memories. The silent boy who was still five years away

from functional speech now spoke clearly to no one in particular, "Shut up, Jack. Sit down and shut up."

My friend and I looked at each other. *What the heck?!*

Jack continued, "Gloria. Hold him down." A chill came over me. Gloria was an aid in Jack's preschool class.

Jack had jumped down the timeline, taking my friend and me with him. We were suddenly peering through the window of a class, held who knows how long ago, watching

Gloria press Jack into his chair. I don't think Gloria was abusing him; falling blocks in the classroom could have set him off, or maybe he went berserk for some other reason causing *him* to knock some blocks down. He could have been a danger to himself and others, and Gloria was protecting him. But the school had never mentioned an incident to me. So maybe this wasn't unusual? Was he often treated this way?

My friend and I sat transfixed as Jack stared into the middle distance, fully engaged in the memory. The feel of the room had changed. My friend's daughter walked over to climb onto her lap.

"Sit down. Sit down. Playtime is over." His voice brought tears to my eyes. My little Jacky Boy who couldn't answer, "How was your day," now transmitting a perfect slice of some afternoon in his past. It was both heartbreaking and spooky.

15

Station KCAJ

Don't you love it when the school's instructional team calls you in to discuss behaviors you've never seen at home? Every day at X o'clock he's doing Y. Until Z occurs, he will not return to task. Why is he doing this? What changes in the home may be causing him to act out this way? What steps are you taking to stop it? Total barrage-o-thon. If real life came with subtitles, you might see:

"We don't know what to do, so we're hoping this is your fault somehow."

Your head-scream is so loud that you're about to burst apart. *"What do you want from me?!"* You've never seen this behavior! You didn't witness the events surrounding this behavior, so how can you possibly offer the school any insights? And how can the school expect you to intervene on a behavior that never occurs in your presence? I get that they're frustrated. I realize, too, that they have seen us pull amazing rabbits out of impossible hats over the years. But, you know. *We're not really magic!*

BATHROOM BREAKS!!!

Jack was in second grade when I got called in for a "team meeting." The subject: Bathroom Breaks. ("Dun-dun-duuuuunnnnn!" Lightning bolt!) Jack was potty trained by this point, but he wasn't yet verbal, so correcting his behavior was tricky. Added to that was the fact that his teacher, teacher's assistant and special ed team members were all female. This limited their ability to intervene.

I offered, "I'm female, too! Ha-ha. Ha-ha-ha." Nothing; not a smile among them. The teacher brought her chair around to the front of her desk while her assistant and the SPEDs team sat casually on student desktops. I was offered a chair so tiny that the nameplate on the teacher's desk was now above my eye-line. I'm pretty sure that was intentional. Bathroom Breaks. ("Dun-dun-duuuuunnnnn!" Lightning bolt!) I'm guessing they were a big deal at this school.

Am I really that old? Because back when I was in grade school, kids went to the restroom during recess as they pleased. If they needed to go in between recesses, they raised their hands for permission to leave class. This urinary anarchy has since ended. At my son's school, kids now leave the classroom at specific times of the day to line up in the hallway. They then march down to the restrooms together, whether kids need to go or not. After a set number of minutes, they all leave the restrooms and march back to class.

Or, so it seems, all but Jack. That is why I was summoned to sit in this tiny chair. Jack, I was told, wasn't returning to class with the other students. Jack, I was told, was more interested in staying behind in the restroom. (Maybe the seats in there are bigger...)

So here we go again. I'm now expected to solve a problem I've never seen and that is happening only on school property. Even if I left work every day to be present in the hallway during the Great Bathroom Marches, what could I do that they couldn't already do themselves? Hello! Someone needed to remind Jack that it was time to return to class. But all my suggestions were immediately vetoed.

Female aid enters restroom after all students, but Jack, have exited? DENIED

Jack is paired up with a male classmate who prompts him back to class? DENIED

Male custodian enters to coax Jack out of restroom? DENIED

Female aid calls in through restroom door without actually entering? DENIED

Situation is remedied by overdue parental involvement? APPROVED

So, yeah.

Channeling Jack

I left the Second Grade Room Number 7 and walked down toward the restrooms. The lower grade classes along this northern hall had all been dismissed, but the hubbub of the upper grades, still in session along the south hall, echoed across the school. I pushed on the door to the boys' restroom. Inside, the lights were on and I could see clusters of used paper towels below the sinks; the custodian hadn't made his rounds yet. "Hello? Is anyone in here?" No answer, but entering while school was still in session felt weird, so I hesitated.

What was I even looking for? In case I was caught, I should probably be ready to explain myself. I quickly imagined being Jack in a public restroom and made a mental list of problems I might have:

Things That Might Prevent Me (Jack) From Leaving The Restroom:

☑ Flush handles that are difficult to find/grasp/push.

☑ Tricky door latches forcing (me) to crawl out from under the stall.

☑ Faucets that don't turn off/won't stop dripping.

144

- Clothing getting snagged on broken latches.

- Slippery floor causing (me) to walk very slowly.

- Restroom too small to digest a full classroom of kids marching in at once; kids pushing and jostling each other. (I) may be pressing (myself) into a corner until everyone else is gone.

Good. I guess I was ready. I took one last look up and down the empty hallway and walked in.

It was fairly roomy inside. Twenty-two kids in the class, roughly half of them boys? I couldn't see a problem. The smell might bother him, though. The room was an odor trap, formed by a mosaic of one-inch tiles that covered both the floor and walls almost to the ceiling. The potent combo of urinal cake and pee built up in the nose. It was better near the sinks: Here, a woody smell of wet paper towels mixed with the sweet scent of soap.

Was there anything that might grab him? As I walked around checking handles and latches, each click of my shoes bounced crazily around the room. The sound shredded repeatedly through its own echoes as it faded, until you could no longer recognize it as a footstep. Maybe that was a problem?

I yelled toward the ceiling, "I am a bunch of boys screaming and talking loudly!"

The room exploded with echoes, pummeling the walls, bending, distorting and slowly diminishing. It was so bad that I laughed, causing another burst of echoes.

This was definitely a problem! But I'd expect it to drive him *out* of the bathroom, not keep him *in* it. I walked back to the sink and stood, imagining myself as Jack. Why did I want to stay in here?

The room was cool and mildly humid. "Dense," was the word that came to mind. There was no natural light, which Jack normally found disorienting. There were no sounds from the neighborhood; no cars or birds. The room was utterly unplugged from the outside world. In summary: It was everything Jack hated!

But there *were* noises...

Now that I'd stopped clicking around in my shoes, I could hear them; clear and strangely near-sounding:

- ☑ The clatter of lunch trays being cleaned and stacked.
- ☑ A sink sprayer "chunking" on and off at intervals.
- ☑ A lively conversation in Spanish.

These sounds were being piped into the bathroom through the ... well, the *pipes*!

A big burst of laughter travelled across the school to me from an upper grade class. Several knowing "oooo's" were in the mix. One mature voice calming everyone down.

A single "buzz" was followed by an announcement from the Principal reminding kids to turn in their fundraising packets. The bathroom had no speaker, but it didn't matter. I could hear this announcement perfectly as it travelled through the pipes and released itself into the echo-chamber of tile. My ears tingled.

This is why Jack stayed here.

In another bathroom somewhere, a toilet flushed and water wooshed deep through the system. Chairs scraped floors even before the bell rang, dismissing the upper grades. Then came a rush of kids' voices, cupboards banging open and shut, feet stomping in every rhythm and direction, and door bars thumping downward.

Within the melee, I could hear distinct conversations. A girl who hates her sister's new cat. Another claiming she raised more money than anyone else in the fundraiser. Two boys racing their lunch boxes along the wall, both claiming victory. There was only one word to describe it all: *Cool!* Now a voice said, "What are you doing?" It sounded older, like perhaps the custodian, and...

Oh.

I looked over to find him standing behind a maintenance cart, staring at me. "I was just leaving," I said. (See? He was the perfect person to fish errant souls out of the restroom!)

My Report to the Education Team:

Jack likes being in the school restroom. The play of sound through the pipes is more interesting to him than whatever may be happening in the classroom. I can't tell him not to stay behind like this: He's nonverbal and will not understand me. The prompt to return to class must happen at the same place and time that compliance is required. Know that I will not be available to come to school every day to provide this prompt. Surely someone already on campus can do this. That said, you might allow Jack a few minutes alone in the restroom before sending someone to fetch him. The echoes in the bathroom are not just fun; I suspect they're stimulating Jack's intellect. Until he is able to understand classroom instruction, these bathroom breaks may be the most informative part of his day.

22

Get Your Game Face On!

Remember those drama geeks in high school? The ones that bantered in obscure movie dialog?

Drama Geek A: Stop! Who approacheth the bridge of death?

Drama Geek B: T'is Arthur! King of the Britons!

DG A: What is your quest?

DG B: To seek the Holy Grail!

DG A: What is the air-speed velocity of an un-laden swallow?

DG B: Which do you mean? An African or a European swallow?

You: (Face-palming) Just pass me one of the handouts already.

Those geeks might be pulling down $200k at Google by now. Depressing. But I'll tell you what: Our kids are doing something far more impressive, because they don't recognize the words they're saying. They might as well be reciting films in Chinese. I'd like to see the Drama Geeks do *that*!

Clink!

Let's get a refill!

So, this brings us back to echolalia. If your child is engaging in echolalia, you've got it made. Echolalia is an open invitation to play, and play is the building blocks of human interaction.

YES, I KNOW THAT SOUNDS LIKE THE EXACT OPPOSITE OF WHAT I JUST SAID IN AN EARLIER CHAPTER!

I'm an mom with no credentials who hasn't the slightest clue what she's talking about. Consistency is the least of my failings.

Anyway, the difference here is "interrupting" your echolalic child vs "engaging" him. Just ask my old Tokyo roommate Lori.

Sorry, it was "Loree" with two "e"s.

Something about Japan, girlfriend. I don't know what. But half my roommates there were sleepwalkers-and-talkers. And Loree had a thing about beetles, so of course she accepted a contract in Japan where beetles are numerous, huge, collected, traded, trapped, whirled around on strings, and sold live in department stores. (Yoko Ono even married one. Ha-ha-ha, okay, that was bad.)

Three times a week minimum Loree would sleepwalk right over to my bed and wake me up to complain about beetles.

Irony Appreciation Pause: She's asleep, but she's waking *me* up.

"I can't reach the light switch because of the beetles."

"I think the beetles took my toothbrush." (Gross!)

"They're on the ceiling over my bed. I'm afraid they're going to fall on me."

"They're climbing up out of the kitchen drain."

That last one may have been real. But for the others, what could I do? Loree was looking me right in the eye while sound asleep. So I'd just lie there waiting for her dream to change directions and lead her back to her bed. It wasn't a speedy process.

One night, I was dead tired. In addition, I had a 5:30am call at a studio in Setagaya, which meant I would have to be on the first subway at 5:00 which meant I would have to get up at 4:00, and I really wasn't in the mood for Loree's bug obsession. At 1:20am, she shook my shoulder. "I can't get into the bathroom. The beetles are blocking the door."

I groaned, "Let's sweep them up."

Instantly, I regretted speaking. Loree's face changed; I could see her internal "sleep elevator" rising up the shaft. But then it stopped. It was like the elevator had opened its doors on a mid-level floor. Loree stepped back from my bed and turned toward the bathroom. "Can we get all of them?"

Intrigued, I quietly got out of bed. "Sure. We can dump them out the window." We lived on the 9th floor of a building that overlooked a two-story expressway. Those imaginary beetles would be mush.

"The broom is by the door."

"I see it." I walked around the tiny apartment placing my voice where it would make sense as I spoke. "I'm sweeping them up and walking over to the window. I'm shaking them out of the dustpan now. They're falling. Cars are running over them. Lots of cars and a bus. Now I'll sweep up the last of them."

"One is hiding by the cupboards."

"I got it."

"Did you get the ones under the table?"

"Getting them now. Out the window, all of you."

Loree was quiet.

"They're all dead now. Would you like to see?"

Loree didn't approach the window, but her dream may have brought the window to her. She looked down, searching, and seemed satisfied by what she saw. She turned and shuffled back to bed.

Oh, mama! *Yes*! Do you see what I'm getting at? I engaged Loree without waking her up! *That's* what we want to do with our kids!

Here are a few ways I've succeeded engaging Jack in echolalic play:

Engaging Echolalia — Drama 101

Join In! When our kids are reciting a movie scene, we can tap our inner thespian and memorize lines of a lesser character: Not Woody or Buzz, for instance, but maybe Ham. Then we can sidle up next to our kids as they're doing the scene and maybe throw in some silent reactions (What?!! Ha-ha-ha!! Nooooo!!!) as appropriate, to signal that we're playing too. When they get to one of our lines, we can point to ourselves and say it, then point back to our kids to let them know we're done. Like with Loree, we don't want to pull them all the way out of their mental zone. Keep it short, keep it light, and for kiddos that don't do well with eye contact, it might help to stand side-by-side with them.

Then we just follow our children's signals. They may want us to keep going! Awesome! We now get to memorize every scene our kiddos love! If they squawked at us, we back off and maybe leave a treat so when we try again next time, our interruption is associated with a treat. (Yes, that's devious. So what?) If we need to be mute players for a while, that's fine. We can be the utterly minor character that scurries across the screen in front of our kids, like Jacques, the clean-freak shrimp in Finding Nemo, or the cockroach pet in Wall-E. We can take it as slow as we need, no one is timing us! (I'd recommend against choreographical free-lancing, though. The movements should match the movie and occur right on cue.)

Engaging Echolalia — Drama 102
(Prerequisite: Engaging Echolalia — Drama 101)

Mixing It Up: I've memorized hundreds of lines from Jack's favorite movies over the years. As he grew older, I used individual lines outside of echolalic play and switched one or two words in it. This was a great way to stress new words for Jack and to help him understand how the meaning of a sound stream (sentence) could be modified by changing a single element (word) within it. A few examples off the top of my head:

☑ In "A Bug's Life" Flick says, "I know it's a rock! You think I don't know a rock when I see one?" Before putting on his shoes, I've waved a sock at Jack and said, "I know it's a sock! You think I don't know a sock when I see one?"

☑ In Monsters Inc, Roz says "This office is now closed." She brings the shutter down on Mike's hands, causing him to yell, "Yeowwwww," which is so great that it's hard not to use. At bedtime, after completing our usual routine, I've paused in the doorway and said, "This door is now closed," and pretended to close it on my own fingers, causing me to yell, "Yeowwww!" I've also closed, "This refrigerator," "this laptop," "this cupboard," "this dryer," "this book," "this drawer," "this microwave," "this closet," and "this dishwasher." It was a favorite.

☑ In Toy Story, Woody tells Buzz, "You are a child's plaything!" The music in Woody's voice here is irresistible. I've used it tons, like while coating Jack's toothbrush with paste, saying, "You are a child's toothbrush!"

☑ The Lego Movie has a fake TV show in it called, "Honey? Where are my paaaaaants?" While laying clothes out for Jack in the morning, I've said, "Honey? Where are Jack's paaaaaaants?" This was followed with, "Honey? Where are Jack's..." fill-in-the-blank, as I set out undies, shirt, socks, shoes and jacket.

☑ Frozen's Olaf introduces himself by saying, "Hi! I'm Olaf, and I like warm hugs!" I've mixed that one up at dinner time by saying, "Hi! I'm Olaf, and I like warm rolls!"

☑ In Tangled, Flynn Rider sees the wanted poster and exclaims, "They just can't get my nose right!" In the bathroom I've pretended to be exasperated over hair brushing and looked at Jack in the mirror, saying, "Mom just can't get my hair right!"

I could provide a thousand examples. Jack loved this game. We still play it today, even though Jack is now verbal. He comes up with his own, these days, and it's hilarious.

23

Intensive Training

Among Jack's collection of talking toys, poised in the center, with a spotlight shining gloriously upon it, was a Talking Thomas the Tank Engine Train Set by Tomy[4]. This awesome $60 toy looked better out of the box than it did in the package photos. There was a talking engine, two carriages, maybe twelve feet of track, a station building, a platform and bench, and a drawbridge that closed as the train rolled over it. Thomas whistled, played his theme song and spoke four phrases from the show while speeding up, slowing down, stopping for passengers and starting off again. It was magnificent! The crown jewel of Jack's toys! Until I tiptoed to the garage late one night and crammed it into the trash.

Let me back up:

By Jack's fourth birthday, he was a big brother. All the stress that a first new sibling brings on a family was exacerbated by Jack's inability to talk about it. He didn't really know who this baby was, where she came from, and why nobody had come by yet to take her back. So I wanted his birthday to be great. This talking Thomas train seemed just the ticket, and Jack did indeed love it. No other

---

[4] The Talking Thomas the Tank Engine trainsets sold by TrackMaster are different than the ones originally sold by Tomy, which have since been discontinued. The smaller wooden Thomas-series trains also now feature several talking models.

present that year came close. And that would turn out to be a problem.

Because the train, it seems, was built to withstand about 60 hours of use before the trigger that activated the sound files began giving out. Sixty hours will last most children maybe... what... two months? Not long for a toy, that's a given. But an AutiKiddo *will burn 60 hours up in a week.*

Our ride to double-hockey sticks began on day seven when Thomas skipped a phrase. I was 30 feet away unloading the dishwasher, and the sudden, loud squawk from Jack caused me to drop a glass. I froze and listened, hastily analyzing the situation. Beep-beep-beep-beep:

- ☑ Jack playing with Thomas.

- ☑ Train motor running.

- ☑ Music off.

- ☑ Batteries < 3 hours old.

- ☑ Only squawked once. Situation not yet out of control.

- ☑ May enter kitchen for help.

- ☑ Broken glass clean-up now top priority.

- ☑ Baby monitor quiet.

Then I heard Thomas toot, and the music resumed. False alarm, everything was fine. But it would be so only for another few minutes. I had barely swept up the glass before Thomas was skipping phrases willy nilly. The music stopped, started, hitched and stopped. Jack went total Tasmanian devil, and because that's not stressful enough, as I left the kitchen, the baby monitor now exploded.

If you are joining us today from a neurotypical household, yes, I did assist Jack before checking on the baby. Jack was in danger, the baby was only disturbed from her sleep. And no, bringing the baby with me as I helped Jack would not have been a happy medium. Are you nuts?! Do you grab your baby and bring her with you to put out a kitchen fire?!

Jack shrieked, swatted at me, pounded his head and grabbed at the train as I tried to check it for breaks and debris. Even though the batteries were decently new, I changed them again (which required a tiny screwdriver. Ergh! I hate those things! Toy manufacturers must *want* us to go bonkers!) When my high-level trouble-shooting efforts failed, I turned to Jack and initiated the Bear-Hug/Remove-From-Scene/Redirect procedure. Today's mega meltdown required the enhanced BH/RFS/R+treat.

This is why we never get anything done, my friend!

With Jack tucked away in his room enjoying a video and cereal bar, my next task was to prevent "accidental reengagement with the problem activity." I dragged the trainset — track and all — to my closet and sort of threw-folded it in to hide it.

Now I could check on my baby. What a patient angel love. Don't be startled, Momma just has swat-head-hair.

At this point I still innocently thought the train was defective. I boxed it up that evening and took it to Target, where the store exchanged it without question for one of the three other train sets they had in stock. The next morning, Jack found the assembled train that was waiting for him in the living room, and dove right into a full, squealing flap-fest. "All fixed," I said cheerfully. And it was . . . for another six days.

"Ouch, that's a nasty scratch on your neck," observed the Target returns clerk.

"My son loves this trainset and went berserk when it stopped."

She looked at the box then back at me, confused. "Didn't you just return one of these?"

"I did. They both stopped working after a few days. I'd like to try my luck one more time."

"Certainly."

The return and exchange policy at Target has improved my life so much that at times I nearly snivel with gratitude!

The following week, the returns clerk politely ignored my black eye. "Another bad one?"

"Yeah."

She rang the refund through to my card and apologized. "We stopped carrying this trainset. The store out on Forest Pass may still have one in stock." We exchanged a look of mutual understanding: My returns had caused Target to drop the toy, and I was desperate to buy another one. "Do you want me to call and find out?"

"That would be great."

They had seven in stock at the Forest Pass Target! Such riches! I could sustain my son's passion until Christmas!

But no. Returning to the Forest Pass store the following week, I found that the entire stock had been pulled. "Try Ross next door," the returns manager suggested. "They have a few Thomas items." Then he smirked. "Split lip, huh? What does the other guy look like?"

The following week, Ross refunded me for the train I bought the week prior, but they wouldn't sell me a replacement. Was that some kind of challenge? Limber up, crack the neck, bring it! I bought and returned one trainset at each of the three Ross stores in town. Boom!

But then the pickings got slim. Walmart never carried this train, and Hobby Lobby had refused further shipments. (Wait a minute… that can't be *my* fault! I never purchased one at Hobby Lobby…!)

I found one at TJ Maxx which I bought and returned. I also found one at Big Lots, but it had been opened and taped shut again. For all I knew, it was one of my returns! Then, I kid you not, a family at Burlington bought the last one in the store while I stood there watching. The boy skipped out the doors with his parents, so happy. My eye started to twitch. If I'd had the cash, I would have gone after them and offered them twice the purchase price right there in the parking lot.

Maybe this wasn't healthy. Look at me! Why was I going to so much trouble to buy a week's worth of peace in my house when I knew how badly that week was going to end? That's it. I was done. Jack had plenty of toys to play with.

On the way home I spotted Marshalls and made a last-minute, tire-smacking, curb-jumping swerve into the drive.

A worker on the toy aisle was pulling items from the shelves and loading them onto a large rolling rack. Among the jumble was a Talking Thomas trainset. "Are these clearance items," I asked the worker.

"They were. Now they're nothing." He stood and stretched his back. "We're resetting this whole section. Excuse me." He pushed the rolling rack across my path, turned the corner and headed toward the door to the warehouse. And there I stood, holding the trainset that I had quietly slipped from the rack as it rolled by. Tee-hee-hee!

The checker couldn't get the toy to scan, probably because it had already been removed from the database. Gulp. I tapped my fingers nervously as she put on her glasses and manually punched in the clearance price one... number... at... a... time....

Then I was free, running across the parking lot to my getaway vehicle. Muah-ha-ha! But seriously, what was next? Armed robbery? This was absolutely the last time I was replacing this Talking Thomas trainset!

The next morning I sat with my daughter and a cup of coffee, watching Jack enjoy his train. He had every statement, toot, chug, and screeching-of-breaks memorized. He dashed around — kneeling, laying — squinting at the toy from every angle with finger-flicking intensity. No toy was ever more loved. A week later I would be "hiding it" forever in the trash, but so be it. Life's pleasures are fleeting.

24

Cranial Configurations and Other Wild-eyed Theories

Your kid's not verbal yet and he's how old? Five? Eight? Sit down and stop chewing your fingernails; you may need them one day to scratch out somebody's eyes. We've all been there, sister. Oh, let me introduce you: You, this is everybody. Everybody, this is You.

"Hiiiii!"

See? It's common. In fact, if it weren't for language delays, a lot of us never would have bothered to go get a diagnosis in the first place. Am I right ladies? They're all nodding.

Personally, I think the longer your child's is language delayed, the smarter you child is. I have no science to back that up, but I see it like this:

Imagine you have a 3 year old that can play the piano perfectly by ear. If you stop that kid and force him to learn to read music, you're going to be fighting him tooth and nail, and probably killing his love of the piano. Conclusion: You're better off leaving him be.

Same kid, now he's ten. He can play a dozen different instruments, and anything from symphonic to jazz and rock 'n' roll. Nobody can touch him, and he still doesn't read music. Does he want to learn? Yeah, a little. Not so much to help his playing, but to better convey his ideas and coordinate with other musicians. So now perhaps it's worth it to him to give these black dots a gander. See what I mean?

Boom! I'm brilliant. Doing actual research would just slow me down.

Now, I love languages. I love them, love them, love them. I mentioned before how I travelled for work throughout my 20s, right? Well one of the things that struck me back then was how I could jump-start my knowledge of a country's culture by reviewing its language. The things and attitudes that are important to a culture end up getting more words generated about them – I'm sure, for example, you've heard that the Inuit have a boatload of words that describe "snow." (I don't know if it's true, but everyone says it.) Where words are sparse or nonexistent, the culture develops a blind spot. The word "no" in Japanese, for example, is so bald-faced and confrontational that it's rarely used alone. Whole sentences must be wrapped around it, like towels, to keep it from scalding the recipient. And that's if it's used at all. What you're more likely to hear are sentences that deflect away from "yes." Here's an actual conversation I had with my Japanese agent about a glorious three-day job she had booked for me on an island paradise.

Me: "Woo hoo! I'm going to Saipan this weekend!"

My Agent: "I'm not sure, I think perhaps it is cancelled."

Me: "What? It was on the schedule this morning! What happened?"

My Agent: "It looks like this weekend is clear now, so you have the opportunity for another job or for just having fun." She would then end this kind of unsatisfying conversation with, "*Desukara*. So that's why," which was especially infuriating since the "why" of things was never addressed at all!

(In this case, the "why" turned out to be named Tina Butler, a new arrival from Australia. She took my job before she even unpacked, and was very un-Japanese about rubbing it in for the next few weeks.)

The point being, the Japanese culture is formal and conflict-avoidance-seeking. Demanding a straight answer to a straight question is a good way to end a relationship. *Desukara*.

Have a slurp, because it's pop-quiz time:

Imagine a language that has only one word to describe "human affection." English, of course, is bursting with synonyms: Love, adore, dote, like, fondness, care for, attachment, endear, etc. But this language only has one, while it also has a dozen words to describe "duty." Okay? (I'm making this language up, so don't bother trying to Google-cheat.) Here's the question: Do you think its companion culture would have arranged marriages, and do you think those marriages would be happy?

Let's have 30 second on the clock while the Jeopardy music plays...

Times up!

I would answer, "Yes," to arranged marriages, and "Yes," that they would be happy. I would even say that nothing else would be literally *thinkable*.

Good job, shake it out.

The second important feature of language is sentence structure. Sentence structure is like a mini dictator in our heads. It tells us how to organize our thoughts, how to define what we're feeling, and how to adopt the appropriate social relationship during the exchange. Let's take, for example, something as simple as asking someone to hang up the phone:

1. In Spanish you might say, "Please hang up you the telephone." Note the hint of accusation with the use of "you." It's not clear, though, who it is that's accusing "you." It could be the speaker, or it could be all sensible people on God's green Earth. It's up to "you" to decide how guilty "you" should feel.

2. In Japanese you might say "Honorable telephone call concluded please." Now neither "you" nor "I" are mentioned, so "you" has no need to feel shame — especially since the call was deemed "honorable" — and "I" remains blameless should the hanging up of the phone result in disaster.

3. In German, you might say – and this one's my favorite – "Up the telephone tell I you please to hang," The two-word phrase "hang up" is reversed and split apart, with the rest of the sentence suspended perilously in between. It specifies very clearly that "I" is the one addressing "you" to perform the phone up-hanging. There's an implied pecking order: "I" is in charge, "you" is at fault and expected to comply at once. Also, "I" bears responsibility for any post up-hanging fall-

out.

It's so awesome! I just want to pinch the fat cheeks of these sentences!! And it's like this for every language: They each have a unique set of words and a unique sentence structure, which together forge a culture with a distinct intellectual mindset. It's no accident that some languages produce bumper crops of scientists, while others can claim many of the greatest artists the world has ever known. This is one of my favorite topics, and I could really go on and on. **But here's the million dollar question:**

If language shapes the way our brains value and store information, what happens to the child with language delays?

Does the nonverbal child's mind have no internal structure? If not, how does he sort through the tons of data his five senses take in all day long? With my considerable background and expertise (harrumph!) I've concluded it must be *nearly frickin' impossible*! Like trying to clean and organize a garage that doesn't have any shelves! And while your child is hard at it — sorting, clearing some space, and maybe using some empty boxes for stacking — people keep pulling into his driveway to dump another load of junk through the garage door! Well, gee! *I'd start pounding my head, too!*

The Culture of Math
More Mindless Nonsense From
Someone Who Doesn't Have A Clue

Jack has tested far behind his peer group all his life. Sound familiar? Now in 6th grade, he's being assigned primarily 3rd grade work. He doesn't ride a bike and still can't tie a shoe lace, which is pretty typical with spectrum kiddos. Jack and other children like him are considered to have pervasive developmental and learning disorders. Before the word was banished from the lexicon, they would have been considered "retarded," which translates simply as "slowed" or "impeded". It implies that the child is not himself "slow," but that he has been slowed down by something that is repeatedly thwarting him. So it's actually a pretty good description.

This is just me speaking, but I don't believe Jack is slow at all. I believe, in fact, that Jack, and spectrum kiddos like him, take in *much more* data than their neurotypical peers, and that they're struggling under the weight of it all. Returning to the garage analogy, imagine each time a truck comes around to dump a load of junk through the garage door, that our kids receive two-to-three times the standard dump's-worth per load. They need serious shelf-space for all this junk *now*! And I think they find that language shelves, with all the additional sections required for inflection, nuance, emotional calibration, homonyms, sarcasm, and all the rest, just take too dang long to build. So they chuck them in favor of something quicker: Math.

Math is considered the universal language because it never changes. A right angle is always going to be a right angle, no matter what country it's found in, which way it's facing, what size it is, what it's made out of, how old it is, or how you felt when you found it. Zero is neither positive nor negative, half of one-half is a fourth, and 10 plus 10 will always equal 20. Math is simple, clean and predictable. It has no gray area, nor is it subject to interpretation or fashion. It has distinct right and wrong answers which cannot be shouted, bullied or manipulated away. It's perfect, and it comes out of the box already assembled.

As the math shelving slides into place and begins organizing our children's brains, our kiddos develop a culture and worldview that's decidedly different from the rest of the family. It's one that is clear, honest, functional and wedded to patterns — which is not a bad way to live. Our maturing toddlers become serious little humans. They are punctual, earnest, task-oriented, and loyal to a fault. But math has no shelf-space marked "feelings." This can leave our kiddos emotionally illiterate, and they're often shocked and disoriented when other humans cheat them, lie to them, or use them to gain advantage against a third party.

According to my brilliant theory, it's not so much that our kids are "disabled" as it is they're *foreigners*. And while behavioral intervention will help them to blend in a little better with us natives, they will forever remain culturally mathematical. But girlfriend, that could be a very good thing. Math-based thinking gives our kids advantages that may catapult them over their peers. I honestly believe this. The trick is getting our kids ready so they can make that jump and land on their feet. We need to push them to become as bicultural as possible, and it all starts with learning "language" as a second language.

Easier said than done, I know.

Thank you! Class dismissed!

Count Your Blessings

Your friends with neurotypical kids can have a hard time getting them to go places. The "I don't wanna" tantrums morph over time into, "Seriously Mom, that's so lame." And these kids often hide or run off to a neighbor's to avoid shots, dental appointments, visiting relatives, and the like. But our math-based kiddos are wedded to the clock. When it's time to go, many of them are ready and at the door, even when the destination is undesirable. What sweet little troopers!

Weird Autism Myth #4

Autistic behaviors in children result from a lack of maternal warmth and attachment

Leo Kanner's 1940's theory on The Refrigerator Mother was debunked and abandoned by everyone – including Leo Kanner – by the 1970's. But over those 30 years, a blame-the-parent mindset took hold, and it continues to linger within this neuropathological field.

For today's discussion, let's put the emphasis on "pathological."

According to our professional betters, no matter how much parents are doing, there's always something more we *should* be doing, and something we're doing that we should have done *sooner*, and something else that we *never should have done* in the first place. For shame! I'll give you a rather "out there" example: Back when Jack was a preschooler, an early childhood educator scolded me for letting him play with his toys using a circular arm pattern that went inside-to-out rather than outside-to-in. Couldn't I see this altering his normal brain processing? !

(Or was it outside-to-in instead of inside-to-out?)

(Honestly, I don't remember.)

But the whole thing was ridiculous[5] and she made this sweeping

---

[5] Over the years, I've not read nor heard another mention of a connection

judgement of my parental inadequacies based on five minutes of watching Jack play. Oh, and the damage was already done, by the way. The school couldn't promise to fix a child that I had so carelessly broken.

She didn't say it quite like this, but, attention people:

That's the way we hear it!

25

Down the Tubes

You know those play area climb-and-slide structures that they have at many fast-food restaurants? Aren't they greeeeaaat... ? Yeah. This is my non-committal face. So call me a Refrigerator Mom after all, but here's the thing: Our kids might find them

---

between autism and circular arm-motion play —inside-to-out or outside-to-in. And trust me, I've been looking. I guess this motion theory that demanded my shame was fleetingly short-lived.

interesting, and they may enjoy watching other kids scramble in and zip out, but they're typically less willing to join the cacophonous clamoring than they would be to skip into a double-Dutch game where the jump ropes had been replaced with live, sparking, powerlines.

Heh? Heh? Am I right?

Maybe I overworked that analogy. The point is, our kids tend to stay out of the tubes. That may be a good thing; not just because of cacophony, but because, occasionally, there's caca.

That said, it crushed my mom-soul to watch my kids — restaurant after restaurant, month after month, year after year — pacing the front of the play structures, but never venturing in. Other children seemed to be having a blast in there. Nothing was more symbolic of my kids' self-banishment than the sight of them literally standing "outside looking in."

So when one day, at our local McDonalds, my three-year-old daughter climbed up the two steps leading to the playland's entrance, she got my full attention.

Just curious: As preschoolers, my kids didn't lean forward and "crawl" into a climb. They'd lean back — relying on me to keep them from falling — as they "walked up" whatever it was they were climbing. Is that an Auti-thing?

Don't ask me why, but I never seem to be dressed right for these sudden Mom Moments. I'd had a meeting earlier and was still in a pencil-skirt suit with 3-inch pumps that now spiked into the rubbery flooring around the play structure. Running on the moon would have been easier! I reached my daughter's back just as she leaned into me. She put both her feet into the tube at once and scooted herself into a seated position. There she sat; right inside the entrance, listening to the echoing shrieks and calls from children located every which way throughout the structure. The expression on her face was a mix of curiosity and horror.

"What do you think," I asked. I put my head through the entrance and called into a tube, "Hellooooo!"

With the experience thus focused for her, she now smiled and called, "Hellooooo!" She was rewarded with a bouquet of giggles from children located who knows where within the playland. Fist-pump for small successes.

Then a pair of kids pushed passed me and charged through the entrance. They scrambled over my daughter. The second one kicked her in the face. Whateryagonna do; they were kids. But my daughter was done.

Crying, she held her arms out to me. I pulled her from the tube and shoe-spiked my way across the soft flooring to set her down in the dining area. She ran straight back to the safety of the table and the half-melted ice cream that waited for her.

No. That was her *brother's* ice cream. So where was *he*?

"Jack?"

As I'm sure you know, losing an AutiKid brings on insta-panic. He wasn't in the dining room or along the front of the play structure. Through the window, I checked the parking lot. The view wasn't full enough; I'd have to go outside to look.

"Stay here, okay?" I told my daughter, knowing she'd comply for less than 30 seconds. Especially since she wasn't listening to me. She was focused on something above and behind me. It wasn't until she laughed that I bothered to turn.

There was Jack in an observation pod on the second level of the play structure!

I saw him, but my brain rejected his location. It was like finding the washing machine in a tree or the sofa in the upstairs bathtub. It was *inconceivable* that Jack had gone into these noisy, stinky, claustrophobia-inducing tubes and climbed his way to the second level. He smacked at the observation window as he spoke unhearable words at me. I forced a smiled and gave him a big wave.

"Hi! How did you get in there," I signed and said.

And how are you going to get out?! No joke! As Jack sat rolling a small Happy Meal car across the pod's plexi window, he seemed less reachable than...

... A gushy love e-mail written during a wine-infused moment of weakness but regretted in the morning, long after the send button was hit, and daring to reread it, you find that it's even more horrifyingly gushy than you remembered. *Noooooooooo!*

Not... that... this ever happened to me.

I'm sorry, what was I saying?

Right. A streak of kids now passed through the pod behind Jack. Jack turned to watch as they headed for the tubed incline to the third level. The hand holding the toy car left the window. A moment later, Jack's face disappeared. If these were the same kids that had rattled his sister, odds were they had rattled Jack, too. He was probably looking for a way out, and I had no idea how to help.

How many tubes connected to that pod?

I stepped back for a better view into the pod. When that didn't work, I pushed some trash aside on a nearby table and climbed up on top to scan the entire second level. Jack's shirt was bright red; spotting him should have been easy. But every small window, play space, netted crawl-bridge, and observation pod along the level was Jack-free.

"Uh... if I could just..."

Somebody's dad was at my feet, moving the table-trash to a tray.

Oh. Maybe it wasn't trash yet. "Were you still eating?"

"It's okay. We'll move." He seemed rattled that a woman in a skirt and spiked heels was standing over his meal. He ducked off, carrying the tray to another table where an unhappy woman sat glaring. I gave her a small, apologetic wave.

That's when a flash of red shirt caught the corner of my eye. I focused back on the tubes and gasped loud enough to turn nearby heads. Jack wasn't anywhere on second level. He was on the third.

Way up in the dizzying, tubular stratosphere was a donut-shaped observation deck and a zigzag of tubes leading to a long, spiraling slide. Jack was busy zigging his way through into the last zag. If he didn't then take the slide, I couldn't imagine how he would get out of there! Nor could I imagine him taking the slide, although I did try:

Spontaneous Child-Channeling Exercise

Come on, Mom... You *know* you do this!

My knees are zigging, my shoulders are zagging. The hard angle on the left side of the tube presses against my waist. The toy car digs into my palm as I crawl along. The yellow tube I'm in is translucent. Bright. It has a small window in it that overlooks the dining room. I look down on a scratched and slightly blurry world. People are eating, talking, swiping at phones and walking around with trays. Adults call out to kids as the kids run every which way. In the middle of it all, my mom stands on a table.

Behind me in the tube structure, I can hear other kids. The plastic beneath me moves slightly as these unseen kids clamor about. It's very warm in here. The air smells like French fries and feet.

Ahead of me, the next tube section is blue. Light does not pass through it very well and it has no windows. As it drops downward and curves, the shadows inside it get darker. I can't tell how long it is or where it's going. Something scary could happen in there as I slip through the dark with no control. I might get hurt or stuck where no one can find me. I don't want to go that way anymore. Can I turn around? The other kids sound closer now. Their voices are confusing me. I'm getting too hot in here and I don't know what to do. I'm trapped. My mom needs to open this window in the yellow tube and pull me out.

I look down. She's no longer standing on the table.

Channeling exercises don't often freak me out like this. I had already climbed down from the table and now spike-stepped across the soft flooring to the base of the spiraling slide. I stuck my head in the bottom. "Jaaaaack!" I called with a musical calmness I didn't actually feel. "I'm down here! I'm at the bottom of the blue slide! Would you like to come down?" I paused, listening. He wouldn't understand my words, but the sound of my voice might be enough to lure him down. Through the long, twisting tube, I thought I could hear Jack breathing. "I will catch you. Slide down to me. I'm right here." Pause.

The slide thumped slightly. Jack may have seated himself at the top.

"Jack? You can slide down to me."

There was a light scratching along the tube, and then the Happy Meal car leaped from the bottom of the slide to fly across the dining room. A small child scrambled over and grabbed it. Grand theft auto in training.

I spoke into the slide again. "Yay, that was fun! The toy car came out of the slide! Would you like to come down too? I'm right here…" And for a moment, I honestly believe he was ready to give it a try, but the moment was squashed.

A voice from the top of the slide said, "Go!" The voice wasn't Jack's.

A second voice joined the first. They both now said, "Go! Go!"

The third voice was Jack's. "Aahhh," was his angry response. This was followed by bumping and shuffling and more Jack complaints, and then a boy, seven-ish, appeared at the bottom of the slide.

One obstacle down, I thought. After the second emerged, I could start grooming Jack again for the plunge.

But unfortunately, Obstacle One ran off to an adult at a nearby table. "Dad," he complained. "Some kid up there is yelling and blocking the slide!"

(Insert curse word here.)

Because our job isn't difficult enough,
right? There it is: Unnecessary public
confrontation by people who don't have a
clue. We all want to hit that brat for
causing whatever is about to take place.

Obstacle One's dad sat up like a roused bulldog. "Where's Deena," he barked.

The boy pointed. "Up there with that kid."

Bulldog rose and strutted over near me, and I knew: He was either going to yell up the slide, or he was going to yell up the slide. Before I could devise a socially acceptable way to stop him, he bent over and *yelled up the slide*. "Deena? Come down!"

"I'm trying! This kid won't let me past!"

Jack now had angry voices yelling from both directions.

"Please don't," I asked Bulldog as he filled his chest with a fresh round of yellable air, but he was locked on target.

"Kid, you let my daughter past or you will be one sorry young man!"

Socially-acceptable now got shoved off to one side. "How dare you talk to my son like that!"

Bulldog stood and looked at me. In my heels, I was slightly taller than him. Weirdly, this made me feel better.

"That's *your* son?"

"Yes!"

"Tell him to get out of the way!"

"He can't understand…"

"Then tell him to slide the hell down!"

"He can't do that either while you're..."

"What, is he, fat?"

"What? *No!*" I'm telling you, girlfriend: Some of the clearest cases of IDD are running around undiagnosed. "He has autism! Shut up for two seconds and listen to what I'm saying! He's scared. And you and your daughter are making it worse by yelling…"

"Autism?!" Bulldog put his hands on his hips and looked at the ceiling in exasperation. "What is it with you people? All of a sudden you're everywhere!"

I'm sorry, maybe there's a good response to that, but what came out of me was: "Oh really? I could have sworn the problem was too many assholes!" It felt good, but it wasn't helpful.

"You know what I think?" He pointed a finger at me. "I think *'autism'* is a new way to describe what you get from *poor parenting!*" Bulldog walked back to his table. Before sitting down, he gestured toward the playland tubes, giving me the full-on Archie Bunker face. "You'd better go in and get him!"

God, I did not want this idiot to be right. But he was right. I was going to have to physically help Jack either back up through the zig zag or brave it down the slide.

One of the counter girls was in the dining room on her break. I gave her $10 to sit with my daughter while I rescued her brother.

Yes my friend. Everything costs an AutiMom more – even a trip to McDonalds.

Removing my shoes and blazer, I entered the tubes.

So here's a tip for you: Avoid wearing pencil skirts when crawling through playland tubes. To get the leg movement I needed, I had to hitch the skirt up higher and higher, until it barely covered my rump. If that wasn't humiliating enough, my stockings left me sliding around every time I moved, but I couldn't just strip down in the McDonald's play area! I forged on; two crawls forward, one slide back. And you know, these tubes aren't meant for adults: Their ceilings are too low, their curves are too tight, and the netted bridges wobble weakly under the weight of... never mind how much. Let's say, "Someone weighing more than 70 lbs." Several times I got myself wedged into weird positions that caused me to panic. How do crews ever get in to clean these things?!

Maybe they don't? I tried not focus on the booger-like smears along the walls.

It took me more than 10 minutes to reach the third level, during which time other parents called their children out of the structure. Through the small windows I could see them all lined up along the edge of the rubber flooring, watching me, like I was a fire fighter going

180

after someone stuck on a ledge — an inept fire fighter sliding back for every two crawls forward. Another day, my AutiComrades, another drama.

As Jack saw me crawl into view, his face lit up. The moment then passed and he began slapping the plexi window in the zag tube: He didn't want me to play, he wanted me to open the window and get him out. He was impatient, which meant that backing him slowly down and out of the tubes may not be an option.

"Hey, Jack."

(Window-smack, window-smack.)

"Do you want to go down the slide with me?"

(Window-smack, smack, smack!) "Ahhhh!"

"We need to go *that* way." I pointed to the blue, spiral tube.

Jack looked briefly, but then he began slapping the window harder. He thought I didn't understand him.

I wished he still had his car. Rolling it down the slide right now might have shown Jack how this dark, curved tube *was the way out.* Scanning our audience, I didn't see the little car thief among them. Not that I could have magically retrieved the car from up here anyway.

Seated at a table with his arms crossed, was Bulldog, flanked by his two obstacle brats. His smirk made me wish the whole structure would tip over and land on them.

Then I noticed a girl standing near the base of the slide. She was only nine or ten years old, but she was watching with more engagement that the others. On a whim, I pointed to her and removed one of my large, cluster earrings. I held it up to the window for her. She nodded, bless her heart.

"Hey Jack," I said softly, tapping the earing against the window.

"What would happen to my earring if I threw it down the slide?"

The tapping got Jack's attention. His eyes followed the earring as I held it up and gently tossed it over his shoulder into the slide. He turned to listen to it scrape its way down, down, down. When the sound stopped, he looked at me.

I smiled and pointed down at the window.

Jack looked down. Standing by the slide, the nine-year-old girl now held the earring up over her head. She waved it back and forth for Jack to see.

I took off the second earring and held it against the window. When the girl nodded again, I tapped the earring to get Jack's attention. "Your turn," I said softly and handed him the earring.

He looked at the girl. He looked down the throat of the blue, curving tube. After a moment, he hurled the earring into the slide. It bounce-scratched down the tube. When the sound stopped, Jack returned to the plexi window and looked down. The girl stood up, now holding both earrings, one in each hand. Jack squealed with delight.

"Shall we?" Jack looked as ready as possible to take the plunge. Helping him turn into a seated position, I slipped my legs around him, held his waist with one arm, and waited until I was sure he understood what we were about to do. "Are you ready?"

Jack squealed again, which seemed a pretty good indicator. With my free hand, I pushed us gently into the slide.

"Look out below!"

And down we went – much faster than I would have wanted. (Stupid stockings!) I found myself dragging both hands along the tube to keep us from flying out the end of the slide. We emerged to laughter and some applause. Jack stood, smiling and flapping, to bask in this approval.

The young girl stepped over to return my earrings. Her name

was Stacey, and I absolutely slathered her with praise for her smarts and willingness to help. No parent was with her; she had walked to McDonalds with her five-year-old twin brothers, and her 14-year-old sister/baby sitter. I offered to buy them all ice cream.

Before I could reach my purse, we were distracted by a sudden collection of voices yelling, "No! No! No!" I looked over.

Jack was at the entrance to the playland tubes, busy crawling back in...

Ever wonder who buys those old-fashioned, calligraphy-laced, glitter-strewn cards with 16 stanzas of text on them? It's Jack.

Yes, he's twelve and still verbally challenged. He's also super visual, so you would think he'd go for the punchy, big-image cards with cartoons or animals on them. But no. Here's the card he just selected for my birthday:

"*Mom,*

"*I learned so much from you. You taught me there's always something to be grateful for, the best thing about laughter is sharing it and there's no limit to how much love a heart can hold.*

(open card)

"*You've shaped my life in so many ways and I feel lucky to celebrate you today. Happy Birthday.*"

He then rudely does the math and hashtags how many years I have left before I'm 90.

26

Labels

Great idea!!

I sat up in bed and turned on the light. It was 3:17am.

Did I dream this? Or had I been awake and thinking? There wasn't much difference between the two anymore. And it didn't matter, this was such a great idea: If Jack couldn't hear the individual words in a sentence – even a sentence he had memorized – he needed to *see* those words; See that they were like… like individual cars connected to a long Thomas the Tank Engine train!

Oh, stop with the fancy phrases, would you? I was not "brain blending" with my son, and Hyper Empathy Disorder sounds like something you just made up. Come on, you gotta admit this was brilliant! And in that moment, there in the dark, before wakefulness fully congealed, I decided I would teach my non-verbal, diaper-wearing, four year old how to read!

My friends all said I was crazy. My mom hung up the phone on me and didn't speak to me again for over a month. Maybe I should have waited to call in the morning…

In the meantime, I labeled the entire house!

"Fridge," "Stove," "Sink," "Cupboard," "Drawer," "Window," "Wall," "Mirror," "Door," "Chair," "Bed," "Desk," "Trash," "Closet," "Fish Tank," "TV," "Stairs," etc. Anything large enough to sport a label got a label, and I didn't scrimp: All the doors were labeled "Door," all chairs labeled "Chair," and all the way up the staircase there were labels marked, "Stair," "Stair," "Stair." It took me the whole day. Finally, to make sure Jack understood what these labels meant, I taped one on each member of the family: "Mom," "Dad," "Jack," and "Baby." Jack's laugh alone made the whole exercise worthwhile.

I began using them while I spoke. Jack's eyes followed as I pointed from label to label. After a few weeks, I taped up some sentences. There was one in the bathroom that said, "Time to brush my teeth." There were two on the pantry door that said, "I'm hungry," and "Who wants a snack?" One on the TV cabinet said, "Let's watch a video." The sliding glass door had a label saying, "Let's go outside." The kitchen telephone had two: "Answer the phone," and "Hello?"

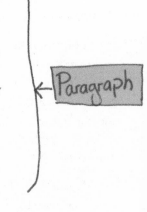

I taped dozens of them around the house. (And because I'm generally lazy, they stayed up until Jack's baby sister was old enough to write up a few of her own. I really need to redecorate….)

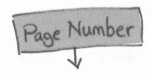

Let me point out that I wasn't trying to teach Jack phonics. I'm not *that* crazy!! I just wanted him to see the separate words as visual blocks with individual meanings. And it worked: He picked them up whole, like Chinese characters. Before long, he was pointing a few of them out in books. YOU HAVE NO IDEA HOW EXCITED THIS MADE ME!! Over the next few months, Jack made real strides in his ability to use and understand specific words, no matter what sentences they were nested in. His therapists were impressed. They asked me questions and took photos of my labeled walls. I felt downright brilliant!

And then everything stopped. Jack reached a plateau and stayed there for a couple of weeks before drifting downward again. Slowly these words I now knew he knew disappeared from his vocabulary, even when I prompted him to use them. The jungle of autism was re-growing over these fresh language trails we had blazed together, and nothing I did seemed to help. Before long, Jack had reverted all the way back to his silent wrist-wave "request" signal.

So What The Heck Happened?

I'm not sure. The problem may have been that I couldn't post labels everywhere Jack went; in stores, the park, the doctor's office, or throughout the neighborhood. Jack is a creature of patterns. Once he realized the label exercise wasn't globally in use, he may have determined it to be a pointless game that we played around the house. And now he was bored with the game. He stopped showing interest as I used the labels, so after a while, I stopped using them. Sigh. I mean, honestly: Who's in charge here? Do you ever feel intimidated by the silent confidence of your spectrum child?

Giving up on my label project deeply bummed me out. Not just because my mom pounced with a few "I told you so's!" It had been such a great idea! It had been working! What could I have done to keep Jack interested and moving forward? Maybe I woke up from that dream too soon to see the plan in its entirety.

There's a thought. If I took a nap, perhaps a new idea would come to me. Sleep sounded so good. Not because I was (yawn) particularly tired or anything. But if I had to go back to the drawing board, that's where I was going to find it....

27

Capital-Z, Triple-Z

Speaking of sleep… What ever happened to it? Even when I have a juicy block of hours for sleep set in front of me (which can be rare for AutiMoms,) I don't seem to get beyond a doze. Instead, I'm mildly dipping and rising throughout the night between dozing and daydream, as the house creaks and the clock in the hallway ticks and the occasional car passes along our quiet street.

And Jack.

I hear him get up, walk around and return to his bed. I hear his lights click on and off. I hear the tiny sound of games playing far away on his tablet. I'm not fully awake, but I'm tuned in, listening for anything that might indicate he needs me.

- ☑ Did he have a bad dream?

- ☑ Is he sick?

- ☑ Is his room too hot?

- ☑ Does he need another blanket?

- ☑ Is he coming downstairs for a snack?

Then his room goes quiet and I drift back into a daydream-doze. REMless in the Rockies. It's been going on for more than a decade, and I swear my brain is dissolving into ooze.

Because I need my sleep. I made that very clear to all parties concerned before having children in the first place. I had an intense, high-stress job at the time as CEO of a visitor center design and development firm. Working 20 straight hours wasn't unusual, but I'd follow it with 12 hours of deep, solid sleep. Wow. That sounds so good to me right now that I'm almost weeping.

Don't think I've forgotten what everyone told me back then! They said, "Don't worry. After a couple of weeks, your newborn will be sleeping through the night." Then they said, "After six weeks, your newborn should be sleeping through the night." When they were still wrong, they resorted to, "Don't worry. He'll be sleeping through the night in four to six months."

That was 145 months ago, and "they" now send my calls straight to voicemail! When I picket their homes at two in the morning, they turn on the sprinklers and go back to bed! Everyone knows that my baby will never sleep through the night! I was double-crossed, hoodwinked and hornswoggled!

There is no way I could work 20 straight hours anymore – with or without the stress! I'm lucky to go five minutes before losing my train of thought or snapping myself out of a micronap. Even in the shower: What was I doing? Oh yeah. Shampoo.

Flash Back, Baby!

Back when Jack was still pretty young (and I was stronger), I held a design meeting for the three contract teams I'd hired on a visitor center project. At the table were the leads from video production, computer programming and thematic décor. For this exhibit, I wanted to achieve a kind of "telescoping" experience as visitors approached, through the use of décor, the environmental sound effects, video displays, etc. Each team's work needed tight coordination with the others, starting with color and texture. So, the teams put forward ideas and began coalescing around cold, heavy colors and thematic walls of wet-looking stone. I interrupted. They were describing a virtual cave, and if we went that route we would probably need to change the music we had selected, which the client had already approved.... Right? That made sense. I found myself agreeing, then I waited for the speaker to make the next point... *completely forgetting that I was the one speaking!* I looked around, and to my confusion, found everyone looking back at me. "I'm sorry, is it my turn?" I asked, "What are we talking about?" Apparently I had "napped" mid-sentence for almost two minutes. Word to the wise: If you're hosting a brainstorming meeting, it's important to bring *your brain.*

I don't run a million-dollar company anymore. I can barely run my household. I stumble around half-awake 24/7, needing more coffee, but never quite getting a fresh pot made. I can no longer trust myself to fold laundry or grab the mail while the tub is filling, because I'll forget until the tub starts filling the house. True story, don't ask. Lack of sleep has been my ruin. Just look at me! I've become that person in front of you in the checkout line at Safeway with mismatched shoes and mascara on one eye; the person who asks you to watch her cart while she goes to grab one last item, then never returns.

I Am Sooooo Brilliant!

Okay, here it is: Amazon.com should sell sleep by the boxful! Am I right?! It could be an Amazon Prime product with two-day free shipping and automatic reordering available. I'd totally buy that!

No, wait! Better: They should make it a digital service; so we could buy our desired sleep units and download them directly to our pillows! Ohmygod, the market for this would be huge! I need to write Amazon about this before I forget... I'm already sitting at my keyboard. So, let's see... Perhaps I should say... Hmm. I could begin with...(yawn)... Wait. I should give the product a name first. How about "Dormir-On-Demand?" .... Wordy... "Somna-Bomb?" That's kind of catchy... Or how about "E-Zzzzs?" Snort. Too cutsie... I wonder if I have any cottage cheese? That suddenly sounds really good to me. I can grab the container and a spoon, then get back to the write-up before I forget where I'm going with this... Huh. Weird... I can't make myself stand. Am I even awake? Oh no, come on. Wake up. This idea is terrifi...

28

Wake Up Call

Her name was Mona Siren. She was loud and flamboyant –
more like a drama coach than a special ed director. Long, loose
dresses hid the orthopedic shoes she needed for the day-long
striding and standing she did. A pound of silver jewelry reinforced
her hands; her graying hair was tied in a long ponytail. The
mainstream kids called her Mama Siren and were often seen
hugging her in the hallway. Staff and parents all loved her.

Jack did not.

When he was in Mona's orbit, Jack's body language screamed
GTFAFM (Google it). He kept a five-foot no-go zone between
them, and defended it by screaming and flapping like a crazed gull.
He never looked at her when she spoke, and when she sat down
next to him, he leaned away until he was nearly parallel to the floor.
I couldn't figure it out – the woman seemed awesome! What could
Jack possibly know that nobody else did?

Wait.

Do Our Kids Have Paranormal Insights?

Laugh if you like, but I know at times you've wondered, too. Our kids can say things with such certainty that we hesitate before correcting them. Or we don't know *how* to correct them. Or we don't know if we *should*. Our day's going along at its usual hyper-speed pace, then suddenly POW! Odd comment from nowhere! Then silence, while we decide if we should laugh or ignore it or call a shrink:

- ☑ You tell your child that today is Great Uncle Robert's 92nd birthday, and your kiddo says, "I'm not going to live that long. I will die on June 3rd, 2089 when I fall off a ladder."

- ☑ Or your neighbor's cat is back on the deck rail again, looking through your window. Your child stares at it for a long time, then says, "The lady lives inside her cat."

- ☑ Or as you tuck your kid into bed, he watches the shifting shadows on the ceiling. He points up with one finger and says, "Someday the shapes will all come together, then the world will start over."

You *know* you've wondered if your child was plugged into some cosmic truth! You think he couldn't *possibly* have *invented* whatever it was he just said, so he *must* be transmitting absolutes from another dimennsion! *Don't lie to me girlfriend, I'm on to you!*

Jack's aversion to Mona meant *something*, even if it wasn't some huge, end-of-the-world insight. Maybe she had "B.O." or halitosis. Mona also hustled essential oils on the side which might have left some weird oil-clash clinging to her that was undetectable to anyone without Jack's super-charged sniffer.

In case she never told you: Yes, Mona *did* sell essential oils on the side. She highly recommended them, and could suggest specific oils for specific traits in specific students… although she couldn't do so during school hours, of course. You could call her cell, or email her at home. Mona had a chronic — cough-mutter-"intentional" — shortage of school business cards. This "forced" her to hand out her essential oils cards as a stop-gap when meeting with parents.

Mona's time was too exquisitely valuable to be squandered on a Level Two case like Jack. She graced Jack with three minutes here, five minutes there, for which he showed inadequate gratitude. The bulk of Jack's time was spent with Tina, who he absolutely adored: tiny, funny, and so flexible that she could stand in front of the whiteboard and draw a picture on it with a marker held between her toes! Jack never had a bad day at school unless Tina was absent.

One such day, I received a call from the school to complain of Jack's behavior. Mona requested me center-stage at once.

Cut to: Me At Home

Now girl, you know we love our kids to bits, but while they're at school, we go giddy from all the freedom. When Mona's call hit my headset, I had an olive oil-soak on my hair, a mud mask on my face, and cotton rolls between my toes to protect my pedicure while I salsa'ed around the living room with the vacuum cleaner to

Ricky Martin. Talk about a buzz-kill.

Mona needed to see me right now. She had a Regional Something-or-other Video Conference in 20 minutes, so this was her window. Right? Like the front door of my home was just down the hall from her classroom! Dream on. I gave her tomorrow at 10:00 instead and promised to do what I could in the meantime to figure out what was going on.

Yep. Yep-er-doo. . . Jack was nonverbal back then, and completely incapable of telling me about his day. Mona knew this, of course, but my "socially-appropriate" statement gave us both permission to end the call.

What I did do later that day was give Jack the physical once-over, looking for scratches, bruises, torn or dirty clothing, bug bites, eczema flair-ups, canker sores, hickies, broken or missing limbs –anything that might explain his inability to comply.

Nada.

I was left with "Jack hates Mona," an impolitic report that was sure to earn me an official frowny face.

But, *hello people!!* I shouldn't *have* to report on something *so excruciatingly obvious!!* If Mona couldn't read the body language of a nonverbal kid screaming GTFAFM, what was she doing running a Special Education department anyway?

Groan.

I was going to be bathed in complaints and given a worksheet of behavioral exercises to begin using at home immediately. Or — and she couldn't recommend this at school, but real quickly — I should check out Bergamot oil. Great for taming aggression. Only $29.95 plus tax. She could have a bottle sent home in Jack's backpack. Which begs the question: *If I bought the oil today over the phone, could I skip tomorrow's meeting?* Ricky Martin needed quality time with me, too you know! I mean… uh… there was so much housework to do.

It's not just me, right?

Do you ever feel like the people around us are on the hustle? They see how desperate we are to help our child "before the window for intervention closes," and decide that we are their personal walking Powerball Jackpot? If only there was a home-based business they could use to suck every last desperate dollar out of our wallets…

Oh wait! There is! *Pack your bags, Raymond! We're retiring in the South of France!* Vitamins, therapies, apps, programs, gadgets, diets, specialized clothing, specialized foods, scented oils, and that woman who wrote that ridiculous book about … (okay wait, that's me. But at least *I* promise *nothing*, and then deliver exactly what I promise!)

Meanwhile, most of the goods and services shoved at us offer no empirical data to show that they will help our child in any way, only the impassioned endorsements of people "just like us." *Tammy from Bakersfield* used this (whatever) for six days/weeks/months, and now her child is giving lectures at MIT, winning Olympic Gold in gymnastics, and ushering in the new Era of Global Peace. Of course, *individual results may vary.* But if you aren't willing to spend $99.95 a month on an auto-renewing subscription to give your child the opportunity to win a Nobel Peace Prize, *doesn't that make you a bad parent?*

Now, I'm not knocking essential oils, here. A lot of people swear by them. My beef is with Mona. None of us should worry, going into a parent-teacher meeting, that the host's main goal is to hustle us out of thirty bucks.

The next day, I arrived at 9:30 in a last ditch effort to score some excuse-data for Jack's defense. His class had gone to the Media Corral in the library to take a reading assessment. Kids sat at separate terminals watching screens, listening through headsets, and busily moving computer mice. The air chittered with clicks.

Over in the corner, Jack sat idle. He stared at the screen without seeing it. One graceful hand rested motionless on the mouse. Approaching him from behind, I winced: I could hear the audio from his headset five paces away! Where were the aides? Mona should've had someone here to prevent Jack from deafening himself. I lifted the headset off.

"This is too loud," I told Jack. He looked up, recognized me, and charmed me with his classic grin-flap combo.

"He was grinding his teeth."

I turned to find the librarian standing behind me — someone who knew zip-all about Jack. She'd apparently been left alone to intervene as best she could. "He does that sometimes," I told her. "We have a protocol in place to stop it. Where's Ms. Morales?"

The librarian swished her hand. "Didn't need it. The more I turned up the volume, the less Jack ground his teeth." She winked as she walked away, as if life among the grade school books had granted her extraordinary insight. *Protocol, schmotocol, baby. You're welcome.*

Well… gotta give her credit for stepping up.

I dialed the volume from 9 down to 3 and slipped the headset back over Jack's ears. I then felt around my purse for a Dum-Dum Pop. *That* was the protocol: Deep pressure of the jaw. Jack would bite down hard into the pop, crush the candy, and then chew up the stick.

Apologies to the Dentist:

"Whole child health strategy" always leaves one provider holding the short straw. Today, it's you.

Ta-da! I found one!

Never mind. It was old, partially unwrapped and groddy with mystery-gunk — basically *me* first thing in the morning. I tossed the dead pop into the trash and headed for the SpEds room where I kept a supply of them stocked for Tina.

The Special Education room was at the end of the main hall, beyond the janitorial supplies closet and opposite the storage room for all the playground equipment. I'm sure this isolation was intentional: SpEds classes can be noisy. Actually soundproofing the classroom would probably have triggered a lawsuit. Now, however, the room was orphaned from the rest of the school. Left unmonitored, SpEds had become its own fiefdom, as I was about to discover.

That one isn't a toast. It's tequila courage. Fair warning.

When I entered the room, Mona was in a one-on-one session with an older child... who she was ignoring. She sat at her desk with her back to the door, typing on her computer. The student had been given a task involving paper and markers. With no one hovering over her, the student had decided to take a break and had moved away from the work table, past an easel, and toward a big window looking out on the mountains. This girl, a skin-and-bones thing about eleven years old, struggled to walk and had to throw each leg forward from the hip. It was determined and painful-looking. She must have really wanted to see out the window.

There was no need for me to disturb anyone – the lollypops were right there on the back counter – so I walked over and picked up the jar.

That's when Mona yelled, "What are you doing?!" She got out of her rolling chair with such force that it slammed the table behind her. I jumped, mortified. That fear of being called out in school never really leaves us. But she wasn't coming for me. She was charging toward the poor girl at the window whose legs now buckled together in fear.

"Eeeee," the girl cried, gripping the window ledge.

"I told you to *sit down!*" Mona grabbed the girl by an arm and pulled her away from the window. The girl's legs didn't move fast enough, or couldn't manage a backwards/sideways stride. She crashed into the easel, taking it down with her as she fell hard on one shoulder. The girl emitted a low, "Maaaa," sound.

Mona bent over the girl, twisted her onto her back and then pulled her to her feet. Perhaps this was the approved method for turning and standing this student, but it looked awful. Mona shook the girl's shoulders as she yelled into her face. "Now look what you've done! Do you see that? That's what happens when you don't listen! Now get back in your chair!" She shoved the girl toward the work table. Some of the student's hair was tangled in Mona's rings, and her head snapped back as her body fell forward. Mona jerked her hand free, ripping enough hair out of the student's head that I could see the strand-cluster from across the room. With one foot, Mona rammed a chair into the back of the girl's knees, causing the student to sit.

That's when Mona saw me standing at the back counter, holding the lollypops. Our eyes locked: She was angry and I was frightened. During the three-second stare-down, our emotions see-sawed: She became fearful and I grew enraged.

I had no idea where I stood legally. Anything I said or did right now would get woven into the final story. It might even somehow become "my fault." I was not backed by a union and nobody was going to hire a lawyer on my behalf. My meager ration of time and money, intended for Jack, might vaporize overnight if I stepped in to help this other student. Morally, though, it was clear: This child literally had no voice. Her mother would never know she'd been screamed at, dropped on the floor, thrown against a table and had a clump of hair ripped from her skull. Tomorrow she would dress her daughter and pack her off for school, confident that she'd be safe and intellectually advanced. How often had this girl been thrown around the room?

What about the other nonverbal students?

What about Jack?

Was this why he disliked Mona?

I hadn't decided to speak when I heard myself saying, "Guess you're out of Bergamot oil."

Mona, however, was busy pretending she hadn't seen me. She ignored my comment and now bent tenderly over the girl's shoulder, speaking to her in that musical child-voice people use with babies and pets.

"What happened to your worksheet," she mewed, sweetly. "Is that it way over there? My goodness. No wonder you got up! You can't reach that, can you?" This "good Mona" routine was intended to guide me back into the pen of happy parents.

Uh, no. That was not going to happen. Did she not get what I just witnessed?! How twisted must she be inside to think her act would "fix" anything? She wasn't just a horrid, conniving person; she might have been unhinged.

Mona retrieved the student's papers and lovingly tucked a marker into the student's left hand, which was still shaking with fear. Was the girl even left-handed? Or did Mona choose that hand so she could keep her back turned toward me? "You know you can ask for help, right?" Mona purred, "That's what I'm here for…"

I felt physically sick. I staggered out of the room carrying the whole jar of lollypops.

We all end up with at least one of these stories. They're wake-up calls, and they harden us in a way we may not like. We start questioning the motives of the people around us who offer to lighten our load. It's sad to have to give up trusting others, but the alternative is ghastly.

Sitting in the empty cafeteria for a few minutes helped clear my head. I pulled out my phone and texted Tina: "5th grd girl w/Downs? drk hair, slim. Idk her name."

A few minutes later Tina responded: "Melodee."

Now the girl had a name. Her plight became personal. I typed:

"Give her mom my #. Say 2 call me."

The next response took longer. I was about to return to the library when the text came in: "Whats up?"

I replied: "U may not want 2 know," and headed up the hall.

The bell rang and kids exploded into the hall all around me.

As I entered the library door by the Media Corral, Jack's class was being herded out through the door near the check-out desk. I'd missed him. His blonde head and Mario backpack jostled among the other students until they had all pushed through to the hall beyond. The sound level in the library dropped, dropped, dropped. As the door closed itself, the big room went silent.

No; not completely silent. Somewhere, a tiny male voice droned. Looking for its source, I walked back toward the Media Corral. Where Jack had been sitting, the reading program still ran. A highlight bar swept across the onscreen text as the tiny male voice read the words. I picked up the headset. The volume had been dialed back to 9.

The meeting with Mona was set to begin in seven minutes. I put the jar of pops in my purse and went home.

Melodee Day + 14

So I spent the next two weeks calling the school every morning to check if Tina was there before I put Jack on the bus. "Obnoxious" was putting it mildly; if the receptionist could have reached through the line and strangled me, she would have. I also typed up a report for the principal that detailed everything I saw that day in the SpEds room. I took my time with this, hoping Melodee's parents would contact me so I could include their feedback in the report. But they never called. Either Tina didn't feel comfortable giving them my message, the message was intercepted, or Melodee's parents chose not to know — all were sad outcomes.

Maybe sending the report wasn't a good idea.

I brought it up onscreen, read it through, and POW! I was rocked all over again by Mona's behavior. If I were the principal I would want to know this had happened in my school. So that was it. I attached the report to an email and hit "send."

Within an hour Principal Larkston was on the phone, nearly hysterical. She agreed to my request that Jack not work with Mona at all, and that he not be left alone in a room with her.

- ☑ Done.

- ☑ Date-stamped.

- ☑ Spindled.

Meanwhile, she would look into this matter and follow up with me as needed. She then paused. "Does Tina know about this?"

Now I paused. Tina knew *something* had happened, but she didn't insist I give her the details. She had a reason for that. My answer might put her in administrative cross hairs. On the other hand, if Tina helped Principal Larkston's investigation, Mona might be gone by Friday.

I went with, "I'm not sure." Fingers crossed.

Melodee Day + 18

My morning pain-in-the-butt call to the school paid off: Tina was absent. I kept Jack home and had him help me decorate the dining room for his sister's birthday. This meant I blew up balloons, and Jack let them go to jet around and land on shelves, in plants, and in architectural crannies (where they would probably stay forever). He also taped a piece of crepe paper to a lamp. When we were done, the place looked festive.

Around 11:00am, I received an email from Principal Larkston:

Good morning Ms. Blackburn,

I'm glad I looked thoroughly into the issue we discussed before involving the school district. It turns out the protocols used with Melodee during the incident you witnessed were as stated on her IEP. All teachers and aids are instructed to use a stern voice coupled with light physical cues in order to redirect this student when she becomes disruptive. It's unfortunate that she fell, but Ms. Siren did not feel this rose to the level of an injury report since this student frequently stumbles as she walks.

Please be advised, too, that Ms. Siren is responsible for every IEP written in this school. It is impossible for her to fulfill this requirement without her working directly with all the students in the special education program. This includes Jack. Going forward, I would encourage you to bring any concerns you have directly to Ms. Siren. That would be the professional and ethical way to handle any differences. If you are not satisfied with the outcome of your discussion with Ms. Siren, only then should you involve me. I trust you will find these conclusions satisfactory.

Respectfully,

Mary Larkston

I reread the note, getting angrier the second time than I did the first. "Satisfactory" my ass! I got up, went to the kitchen, checked on a cake in the oven, poured a fresh cup of coffee and returned to the desk to read the note a third time. I didn't think it was possible, but I got even angrier!

The change in Ms. Larkston's tone was whiplash-worthy! She now deemed Mona's actions appropriate, but my reporting on those actions neither professional nor ethical! *Please*! What protocol, duly approved and formalized into an IEP, would allow a teacher to grab, drag, drop, shake, rip hair from, scream into the face of, and foot-shove a chair into the back of *any student?!* Were these "light physical cues?" No ma'am. Mona threw a total tent of lies over her principal. Melodee, the third person who had been in the room at the time, couldn't speak, so Ms. Larkston was left weighing two different stories. She chose one; the easy one. The one that didn't require her to fire a teacher, or interview, hire and train a replacement. Why hassle the litigation that Mona's exit would generate? Come on! Everyone *loved* Mona. Jack and his mom were "meh." Choosing between these two parties was a no-brainer.

But she made one mistake: She declared she'd be putting Jack back into Mona's clutches, and this mama wasn't having it. I grabbed my cell phone and sent a quick text off to Tina: "Will U B in 2morrow?"

The oven timer went off.

While putting the baked birthday cake on a cooling rack, I heard Tina's reply come into my cell. I checked the screen:

"This phone has been turned in by someone no longer employed by the school district. Please contact your child's school for further assistance."

[Insert curse words. Set volume sufficient to collapse a cake.]

Melodee Day + 19

So Jack now went to a school across town. The move meant giving up bus privileges, and the commute was 45 minutes round-trip, twice a day. But that was okay. The drive kept me focused.

The local autism family list servs channeled good, specific, usable information into my problem from people who had been in my shoes. I got the name and contact information for the District Director of Special Education, a great list of legal-sounding talking points to include in a complaint letter, and an advocate to guide me through the complaint process. None of this was my style, but as the expression goes, Mona drew first blood. We'd lost Tina, some great teachers, a familiar environment, and all the peer support that had surrounded Jack since preschool. Mona was going down.

Melodee Day + 25

With the efficiency of a toaster, my letter to the District SpEds Director popped a response up in three golden, crispy days. Then Grenda Stern's secretary pulled out the plug. She put me on the calendar six weeks out.

Six.

Weeks.

Was the line of disgruntled parents outside Stern's office really that long?

"No," raged the AutiMoms on the list serv. "It's a tactic!" They warned that Grenda Stern ate parents for lunch. Juniper, one of the advocates, noted how the delay pushed my meeting beyond the end of the school year. I'd lose all the anger that drove my complaint. It was my job now to stay sharp, focused and mean. Like a boxer. And I tried, I really did. But summer offers no rest for AutiMoms. Each day serves up 16 hours of stress, five mini-emergencies and one or more big blowouts. From mid-May to mid-August, our Google calendars automatically convert to dog years. That six week wait was ten-and-a-half months in AutiMom time.

Melodee Day + 61

Grenda Stern made us wait 45 minutes. Her "reception area" was barely big enough for her secretary's desk. There were no other chairs. Juniper and I stood in a brown, windowless hallway. "We're supposed to feel defeated," Juniper told me with a thumb's up. She seemed a lot more intimidating on the list serv. Looking at her now in the dark hallway, I was sure: When she has a flat tire, she calls her dad.

By the time the secretary summoned us in for the meeting, my feet were sore.

Ms. Stern looked a thousand years old. She barely glanced up as we entered and took our seats on the other side of her cluttered desk. She pulled a file folder off a stack, opened it and took out my letter. "I see you brought the tree with you."

I looked at Juniper. Juniper looked down at her hands.

I was on my own.

Stern began. "Ms. Blackburn, it seems you have two concerns. You believe a student has been mistreated at Front Range Elementary, and you don't want Mona Siren working with your child." She lowered my letter back into the file. "You've moved your child to another school. Is that correct?" Her bored glare made clear that I was just one in a long line of idiots she had to endure today.

"Yes. That's correct."

"So, one issue is resolved. This other issue is none of your business." She closed the file and tossed it onto a stack on the floor.

Juniper sat forward. "If I may,"

"No you may not," growled Stern. "Ms. Blackburn's letter doesn't state her child was ever mistreated. No other parent has complained. You have no case."

I jumped in. "That other child is *nonverbal*. Her parents didn't complain because she couldn't tell them what had happened to her."

Stern shrugged. "So? She also can't tell them that school is her favorite place in the world. Or that her purple shoes are magic. Or that she wants to grow up to be a snowman. You're not entitled to decide what a nonverbal child wants to say. We're done here." Stern folded her hands and stared at us until we rose awkwardly out of our chairs. No one said, "Thank you," no one said, "Good bye," we just sort of shuffled out through the tiny reception.

"That went awful," I said to the back of Juniper's head as we filed down the hallway to the elevator.

"I've had worse. We stood our ground, that's what matters. That's how you make a difference in the long run."

"Are you kidding?"

At the elevator lobby, Juniper hit the call button and turned toward me. She wasn't kidding; her face was perfectly serene. Suddenly I wanted the past two months of my life back.

She reached in her purse and pulled out her card. "Here. Call me if anything develops."

The doors opened and she stepped in. I didn't follow. How could anything develop from "You have no case"?!

Juniper continued. "I also sell essential oils, if you're interested. Ginger might be perfect for you son's transition to a new school…"

I stepped back and let the doors shut. The stairs were probably faster anyway.

Melodee Day + 594

Seventeen months later, my anger toward Mona was still there, but it no longer kept me up at night. I'd joined the local Arc chapter to up my Disability IQ and to put a few faces to names I'd seen on the list serv. (Not that I remembered many.) I was able to avoid Juniper at a two events. At a third one she cornered me before I could get away. I also had a woman at a check-in table grab my hand as I picked up my name tag.

"You had a child at Front Range Elementary, didn't you."

I didn't recognize her face or the name on her own name tag. "Two, actually. Yes."

"Our daughter went there from preschool through fifth. She's at Pierson Middle School now."

"What's her name?"

"Melodee."

My face must have dropped. I didn't notice how closely the woman had been watching me until now. Melodee's mom let go of my hand and nodded sadly. "I understand they weren't very nice to her there."

"I'm sorry." It was the only thing I could think to say.

Perhaps nothing more was necessary; the stories she'd heard were confirmed. Melodee's mom patted my arm and looked away with a small shake of her head. She then walked off to join a group of ladies across the room.

Lingering Notes

Mona remained at Front Range Elementary until she retired in 2018. A down-chain somebody-who-was-friends-with-somebody posted pictures of the huge party the school threw for Mona. People cried. Everyone promised to keep in touch. She likely walked off with a parting bonus and fat pension that weren't deserved.

Separately, I heard Mona moved to New Mexico with a man 20

years her junior who was rumored to have mild special needs. They bought a condo. I try not to think what that relationship looks like.

29

Top of the Morning

If your kid has trouble sleeping — getting to sleep; staying asleep — you're in good company. Well, I don't know if "good" is the operative term; we're all pretty grouchy. Perhaps I should say "ample," because there are a heck of a lot of us. Right ladies? (Yikes! They're all glaring at me! Maybe we should order a round of coffee?)

Let me take an informal poll right quick:

- Raise your hand if you've tried melatonin.

- How about a weighted blanket?

- Aroma therapy?

- A regimented pre-sleep routine, complete with bath, music and low lighting?

- Have you tried white noise? Jack has a 40 gallon fish

tank that has a nice waterfall sound to it. Not sure if it's helping, but now I'm stuck with the upkeep.

- ☑ How about black-out curtains?
- ☑ Benedryl?
- ☑ A belt of whiskey? (That one's for Mom.)

Six years ago I threw in the towel. Fighting it was too hard on both of us. For whatever reason, Jack's brain doesn't want to sleep, and like the proverbial horse that's lead to water, all I can do is give it the opportunity. So I do. But this horse never seems thirsty.

How Jack functions at all on as little sleep as he gets is a mystery. And yet…

Every Auti-related Oddity Provides an Opportunity!

There is an upside to Jack's sleeplessness: He never fully shuts down at night, so when he wakes up in the morning, he's already in third gear. At the first crack of an eyelid, he's alert, curious, and — best of all — not yet obsessively engrossed in something. **There is no better time in his day for me to access his intellect. So this is when I teach him.** It probably helps, too, that he's trapped in his bed. Muaa-ha-ha!

This "brain window" is open for about 20 minutes, which isn't long, considering everything I would love to cover. It's tempting to try to double-shovel for the full 20 minutes, but I never have, and I sort of want to recommend against it to anyone else. "Sort of," because I have no basis for this recommendation; it's just a feeling.

213

I sense that if I triggered a "that's enough!" response from Jack on Tuesday, his Wednesday window might be only 10 minutes long, and Thursday's only five, then by Friday he might have shut me out entirely. I could be totally wrong about this, but like a lot of us, I've found my AutiMom Instinct to be pretty reliable. So I come into the room organized, work quickly and finish with about five minutes of brain-window-time still on the clock. Jack spends those last minutes digesting the world as he sees fit while I quietly feed his fish and lay out his clothes.

So far, so good, knock wood. Honestly, I could write an entire book on these morning lessons and Jack's incredible ability to absorb and retain information. It's been a humbling journey for me, and we have forged far beyond the original goal I had planned when I first started. That goal had only been to compensate Jack for the advantage that verbal kids had on him: The knowledge of what's coming next.

Uh-huh, Got It.

Verbal kids get the day's run-down from their parents during breakfast while they barely pay attention: "It may look sunny outside, but by noon we'll have rain and sleet, so dress warm. Soccer practice has been postponed till tomorrow. You still have piano, though, and I'm picking you up from school early today for your dental appointment." Verbal kids are like, "Sure, whatever. Who ate all the Cocoa Puffs?"

Non-verbal kids spend every day riding an agenda rollercoaster. They have no idea what's coming next, what will be expected of them, how long it will last, if they're the ones participating or if they're just hostages to a sibling's activity, and if that new thing they just endured is going to be a new once-a-week thing. They can't be prepared when they don't know what's coming, so they don't pack music or a game, they don't bring a drink, they're just stuck with whatever's in Mom's bag, and she's not that reliable. And if they don't know when they're heading home, they can't even manage the urge to poop. They never get to ask who ate all the Cocoa Puffs, and never learn it was *Mom*! All day, every day, they are pushed around like shopping carts, until they start screaming. So honestly, is it any wonder they scream?

My goal was to arm Jack with the information he needed to manage his expectations for the day. I started back when he was in preschool, and it looked like this:

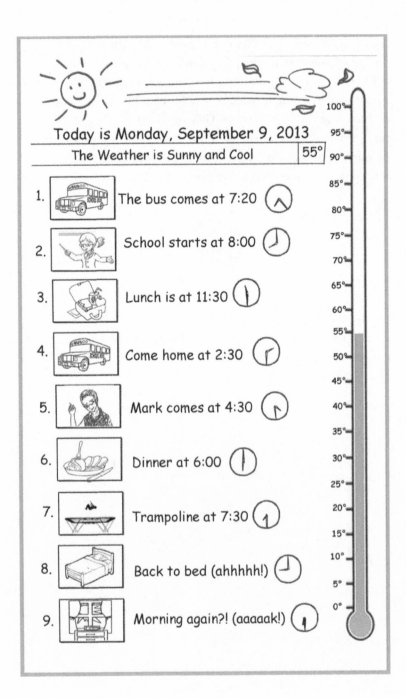

Today is Monday, September 9, 2013

The Weather is Sunny and Cool 55°

1. The bus comes at 7:20

2. School starts at 8:00

3. Lunch is at 11:30

4. Come home at 2:30

5. Mark comes at 4:30

6. Dinner at 6:00

7. Trampoline at 7:30

8. Back to bed (ahhhhh!)

9. Morning again?! (aaaaak!)

Note the hopeful "Back to Bed" at 9:00. Ha-ha-ha-ha! Sigh, wipe tear. All we're looking at here is a white board with some pictures glued to magnets. I kept a shoebox full of these magnet pictures: I had one of me, the school bus, our house, all Jack's doctors, therapists and instructors. I had pictures of food and various activities, other family members, and the bed. If it made the agenda, it had a magnet pic.

Beside each picture, I'd write a short sentence noting the digital time that each event would occur, and finished with a quick analog clock. Easy Peasy

Girl... before you even ask that question: "No, I was not trying to teach Jack how to tell time!"

I wanted to help him pace his day against something constant in his environment with the hope that someday he'd become aware of that constant. I'm talking of course about the wall clock. There's one in every classroom, in most waiting rooms, in every therapy room, and in nearly every room in our house. And the thing is, Jack *did* become aware of the wall clock *almost immediately!* He grabbed the clock concept and held onto it for dear life as he navigated his schedule. He also used it just for fun (see "Tale Number Two" in Chapter Thirteen.)

Our kids are so much smarter than we give them credit for!

If you think something might help your child, go ahead and dangle it out there! You'll be surprised how often you're right!

As I wrote on the morning board, I read the words aloud. I drew a quick picture of the weather across the top, and added a long thermometer on the side of the board — anything that could help him organize his expectations. The whole exercise took less than 10 minutes. Jack would lay there watching, listening, bouncing the binky on his lips. The difference it made in Jack's mood and cooperation throughout the day was **<u>profound</u>**.

Note: That last word was bolded and underlined, so you know I mean it!

I'm telling you! This ten-minute set-aside each morning was the best time investment I ever made (unlike that ridiculous 10-minute parachute-dragging-before-meals business)! Jack's morning board proved its worthiness the very first day we used it!

Okay, sure: Jack's sister got short shrift in the mornings. But she could stumble down the stairs for a bowl of cereal as well as the next kid, right? Really, she wasn't any worse off than her classmates across the street. She just felt gypped, because Jack was getting more. Her grievance wasn't justified.

Er..... uh oh. Yes it was.

Caution!

Your other children are measuring the love and attention in use in your home. They will not compare their parental-doting allowance with whatever their friends receive; they will compare it with what you're giving their Auti-Sib. Of course we both know that you're already using up time that was meant for your job, your home, and your significant other, so... yeah. Until you're cloned, there's little you can do about this discrepancy. Just be aware of it, and find opportunities to slather love on your other kids where you can.

30

What's My Name Again?

This is not a rhetorical question! Most of the people AutiMoms deal with on a regular basis don't use our names — which is charming in a way, but socially disorienting.

Before Jack was born, I was a Vaguely Important Person; not a real VIP, but maybe a lower-case vip. Everywhere I travelled, be it Europe, Asia or the US, there was someone waiting for me to arrive. "This way Miss Blackburn. We have a car just outside."

As Jack began therapy, and later school, *he* was the big presence entering the room. People saw him and responded to him. I was the one behind him holding his backpack. "You must be Jack's Mom," they'd say, if they noticed me at all.

I can count on my fingers the number of times the people in Jack's World asked me my name. Only half of those who did ask ever used it.

And, you know, let's cut them some slack: Our names are on file somewhere, so they don't need to acquire that data from us. Their goal is to link us mentally to a particular child in their care. But... then they're sort of done. The backpack and the mom have both been identified, and business can proceed.

"Bridget, this is Jack's Mom. Can you show her where to put his lunch box?"

"Wait, Jack's Mom! Don't leave yet! We need your signature on some forms."

Welcome to your new life! The world now views us as accessories to our children. Kind of a stature demotion, ain't it. Cheers, ladies.

We all get used to it. And like I said, it has a certain charm. They do this because they are thinking first and foremost of our children, which is exactly what we want, right? I'm at the point where if someone called me by my actual name, I might not realize they're talking to me! But … not to worry: The risk hovers around zero.

Instead, standing in line at the post office, I'll hear someone behind me say, "Can I ask, are you Jack's Mom?"

Leaving campus after dropping off an oversized science project, an aide will run out behind me, "Hey! Jack's Mom! Mr. Chang needs to speak to you!"

Waiting with my daughter at the doctor's office, another parent will approach us with, "Excuse me, my son wants to know if you're Jack's Mom?"

Recently, I gave the keynote speech at a fundraising luncheon for the Arc. I was seated at a table of strangers. We introduced ourselves and made polite chit chat over chicken salad and chocolate cake, after which I was called to the podium to make my speech. When I'd finished, I returned to the table to find my lunch companions standing and applauding vigorously.

"Thank you," I said, sincerely grateful. This was my first big speech, so as we all sat back down, I candidly asked, "Did I say anything useful?"

In reply, I got, "You didn't tell us you were Jack's Mom!"

Sigh. That's when I knew: My son had completely swallowed my identity.

PsychoMom Alert!

31

Pippi Long Stalkings

You know how it is when you think back on something infuriating and find yourself getting as angry about it as you were the day it happened? This is gonna be one of those. I'm telling you. Writing about it is going to be a b-word. In fact... before starting, I'd better order a new keyboard and monitor just in case I break something!

* * * * * * *

Alright. Let's set the scene:

It was early September and the first threads of cool, dry air were now running through the hot afternoons, announcing the coming of fall in the Rockies. Jack was an energetic near-four-year-old, and his freshly-hatched sister did little but snooze. Perfect for them both: Long afternoon walks. So, I loaded up the carriage with the basics: Drinks, snacks, sunglasses, diapers, changing pad, ointment, wipes, trash bag, formula, blankets, hats, sunscreen,... (inhale)... Epi-pen, toys, wallet, house key and phone, and off we went.

I feel like I'm forgetting something…(Snap!)

Baby.

Okay, check.

And off we went again.

"Renovation Man" had moved to a backyard project, so the streets were once again safe to stroll. Did I open the door to his mailbox as we passed by just for spite? Girl, I'm shocked you'd ask such a question!

Of *course I did!*

The other neighborhood regulars were out enjoying the day. The guy with the fake deer was mowing his lawn. The flower garden lady was watering an explosively colorful yard in full zinnia-zenith. New nursing school students had calculated their risk for melanoma and now basked in front of the rental house in lounge chairs. Right next door, Decoration Lady had just changed themes from "summer patriotism" to Labor Day. As we ambled along, I "helloed" everyone.

Red-white-and-blue-truck-guy leaned on his porch rail, sharing a beer with a visitor. Jack scrambled up to the gravel landing to inspect his vehicles. I thanked Truck Guy and his visitor for tolerating Jack's intrusions. They nodded with gruff, Colorado hospitality.

Truck Guy's visitor pointed with his beer can. "What's he got?"

"What?" I peered between the vehicles for Jack. There he squatted, comparing the trucks' undercarriages. His hands were empty. "Did you see him grab something?"

"No," the visitor clarified. "What's wrong with him? His illness. What's he got?"

"Oh." I never quite adjusted to the blunt candor of Rocky Mountain folk. "He's still being tested, but we think it might be autism."

"Uh huh?" The visitor nodded thoughtfully. "Well. That's a shame. He's a handsome boy."

Was I tearing up? Gotta be post-partem. I pulled my sunglasses out of the stroller's carryall and slipped them on. "Thank you. He's actually doing pretty well, so… it's all good."

Of course, it *wasn't* all good. As you surely know, AutiFamilies go through a period of gawdawful readjustment, and this was right in the middle of ours. The diagnosis wasn't firm, Jack's dad and I were near fisticuffs over what was happening and how to address it, the cost of therapy would drive us into bankruptcy before the spring, and my family in California had gone silent. I mean *silent*, the way crickets go mute when they hear an approaching threat. Not one of them would even send us a Christmas card that year. Listen up, people: *Autism isn't contagious. Especially not through the mail!*

There are times when you just need to keep walking.

"Come on Jacky boy," I called and pushed the carriage into motion.

The sidewalk curved around the open space where chipped and rusted signs rasped out warnings like old prospectors on their deathbeds: "Caution: Mountain Lion Habitat," "Beware of Rattlesnakes," and "Bears Spotted in Area." These days, people walked past without a glance.

Beyond this stretch, the road forked. To the right, it wrapped around the hill and entered the main university complex. To the left, it entered the parking lot for the university's theater annex. Or it *would* have entered the parking lot if it weren't for the tight blockade of traffic bollards. So tight, in fact that the carriage wouldn't fit between them.

This was the end-of-the-line for me. Jack, however, would pass through the bollards to admire the cars in this farthest row of the theater parking lot. Between classes, nothing in the lot moved, and Jack was never more than a few yards away from me. I had no reason to feel uncomfortable.

Here She Comes..!!

↓

But today a student walked past me through the bollards. She wore black lipstick and false eyelashes along both her upper and lower lash lines. Her bowl-cut hair was dyed navy blue. She wore a red skirt so short that, with every step, she flashed black undies. And are you ready for this? You could see her maxi pad!

To complete this ivy-league look, she wore black platform boots, and red and black stripped, thigh-high stockings. Yep. Portrait of an American academic.

I was willing to cut her some slack at first: She was headed for the theater building, so maybe this was a costume?

She panty-flashed into the parking lot and marched a few steps past Jack. Then she stopped (dramatic pause). After a moment, she performed a 90-degree pivot toward him. As any budding thespian will tell you, no audience is too small for a performance. "Hello little boy," she said "Are you out here all alone?"

"He's with me." I waved with sarcastic exaggeration. Did she really not notice the woman with the baby carriage as she went by?

She looked at me, and then chose to ignore me as she spoke to Jack, who in turn ignored her as he studied a Chevy 4x4. "You shouldn't be here on your own. Where's your mother?"

"Hello, that would be *me*," I said, getting a little ticked. Sheesh. Where's a mountain lion when you really need one?

She snapped her whole body in my direction, purposefully flipping her hair and skirt. "Why are *you* over *there*," she asked.

I spread my arms across the width of the carriage. "We can't get through."

"Then why is *he* over *here*?" Both her expression and gestures were pure cartoon. She had no concern for Jack; this was street theater. Yet here she was, a buffoonish 20-something, lecturing me like I was her failing kindergarten student.

Teacher, teacher, I declare. I see someone's underwear. Yours!

"Let him do his thing," I said. "He has autism and just wants to look at the cars. I'm right here for him."

"But I don't know who *you are*," She sniffed, modifying her script to capture a new storyline rich with dramatic potential. "You could be some weirdo in the parking lot!"

I couldn't stop myself: "Excuse me, but if anyone here is a parking lot weirdo..."

"Hey little boy, can you tell me who that woman is?" She bent down and tried to turn Jack by the shoulder.

"Don't touch him!"

Yikes! I about to pound my keys all the way down through my desk! Someday I'll have arthritis in my fingers, and they'll trace the damage back to this moment. One more reason to seethe!

Okay. I can get through this. Let me just…

That's better. So where was I?

Maxi Pad tried to turn Jack by his shoulder, causing me to yell, "Don't touch him!"

Jack threw her hand off and bleated at her like an angry goat. He then scrambled away, running deeper into the parking lot until he disappeared from view.

"You meddling *bitch!*"

"I'm calling the police," she countered with utter idiocy. Pulling out her phone, she fast-walked after Jack.

"Leave him the hell alone!" I took three steps in pursuit before remembering my sleeping daughter. Cursing, I went back, unstrapped her and pulled her into my arms. This did not make my

baby happy.

Maxi Pad had followed Jack across three aisles of cars. "Come with me little boy," she said. "Let's go in the building where it's safe." She tried to grab Jack's hand and he went auti-bat-shit on her, which she totally deserved. This may not be how she envisioned her parking-lot-play unfolding. But the key to good "improv" is never saying, "No:" You say "Yes, and," then move with the scene as you develop it — or something like that. Anyway, dragging Jack didn't work, so she decided to "herd him."

Maxi Pad swept her arms to propel my screaming son across the parking lot; a behavior so insane that my eyes refused to believe it. I would have shot video, but *crap!* I'd left my phone in the carriage... along with:

- ☑ $35 cash
- ☑ My debit card
- ☑ Three credit cards
- ☑ My state ID with my address conveniently printed on it
- ☑ The key to the front door of that same address
- ☑ The key to the car parked in front of that address
- ☑ Half a box of Nutri-grain bars — mixed berry (which were my favorite and were rarely in stock at the store!)

This is about when I went berserk.

"Who are you," I screamed. "Are you a student here?! What's your name?! WHAT'S YOUR NAME?! Do you any idea what you're doing?! This is false imprisonment! You are *kidnapping* a *disabled child!*" Good line, right? And maybe even true! I yelled much louder than necessary, hoping someone would come out to help, or at least witness what was happening. "Look at me you idiotic, shitty little maxi-pad-flouting thespian! You are in *big trouble*! Do not doubt for a second that when we reach that building *I* will be calling the police about *you!*"

I was so angry that I almost blacked out — exactly what I told you *not* to let happen, right? At one point Maxi Pad glanced over her shoulder at me and… I don't know. Maybe I was foaming at the mouth? Perhaps she realized I would never appreciate her artistry, or maybe she sensed that her spontaneous script had led the scene down a dangerous alley. Whatever the case, she could see I was dead-serious, and I was close enough to her now to be physically threatening — even if I was holding a baby.

Shrieking, Maxi Pad ditched the script and made a hasty exit stage right, clomp-clomp-clomping in those platform boots and holding the back of her skirt down with one hand.

I continued to screamed "WHAT'S YOUR NAME," after her, but I couldn't chase her any further. I had broken my own Rule Number Five. Both my kids were crying and now needed their mommy.

My loves. I'm so sorry. The horrible freak is gone now. The three of us moved slowly toward the bollards and back out to the street; the kids snuffling and me fuming.

AND I'M STILL FURIOUS OVER THIS POINTLESS ENCOUNTER!!

One pathetic, hideous "student" put Jack in danger by driving him across a parking lot! She had scared him and ruined the afternoon for all three of us! And for what? Self-glory? Boredom? To hone her ridiculous "craft?" Is there some other petty, self-centered motivation that I'm overlooking here? I swear, I'm ready to blow my lid to this day!!

Hang on a second…

There. Tea and a Nutri-Grain bar might soothe my nerves some. But, I'm telling you! I could have *kicked that thespian in her fat, pad-flashing butt!* And *she's* someone I might actually *recognize* if I ever ran into her again. So should that happens, ha-ha-ha! Can you imagine? There she is, standing on the corner just waiting for her Uber or something, and this strange woman walks up and kicks her in the butt? Ha-ha-ha-ha! I'm so going to do it!

32

Life is a Dream

I'm sure you've noticed...

Our kids spend much of their time someplace where we can't reach them. They don't respond to their names. They stare off in the distance as their favorite foods sit in front of them, growing cold. Or they don't notice they've hurt themselves and continue whatever they're doing, even as blood trickles down from the wound. It's like they've mentally jumped into a helicopter and soared away, leaving their bodies parked and idling at the curb.

I don't know what drives our kids to do this. The answer could be something as simple as, "They can." And I'll tell you, there are days when I would give anything to be able to concentrate that fully.

But it has a dark side. I'm sure you've noticed that, too.

The Stuff of Nightmares

Before our kids learn to communicate, they are alone in the dark forests of their minds. It's huge in there, they have no compass, and frightening elements slip quietly among the shadows. There's little we can do to help them, and they can't reason their own way to safety, so they tough it out and learn to accept this inner *Schwarzwald*. Some of them mince forward cautiously, looking everywhere for the dangers they sense are lying in wait; others charge forth with a battle yell as they beat back the mental underbrush with sticks. They're on their own, even when we're standing right beside them. It hurts my heart to think about it.

Better make that a double.

Jack was a mincer. He was on high alert every waking hour – which was roughly 20 a day, as anyone could tell by his eye baggage (and mine).

He also ate next to nothing. My once chubby baby was skeletal by the age of 5. Threats to his mental peace were everywhere: wet textures, windowless rooms, stepping outside without his shoes on, the smell of cooking eggs, the voices of Charlie Brown cartoon characters (weird!), conveyer belts, balls bouncing towards him, a moth flapping around in the room… the list spooled out and dragged behind him for fifty yards! I knew he had reasons for behaving the way he did, but I could only guess what they were. Like the day he stopped climbing a neighborhood play structure.

He LOVED that play structure — all caps, yes ma'am — because of three awesome slides that twirled down from a second-level platform. To get to that glorious platform, you could climb:

1. Stairs (Jack's usual choice),

2. A rope ladder (Jack touched once, never attempted),

3. A short climbing wall (Jack gave one half-hearted attempt on),

4. Or a huge curved ladder that arced up out of the sand (Jack climbed occasionally).

Two-thirds of the way along the curved ladder, kids were no longer climbing up; they were scrambling across horizontally like monkeys; back's curved, fannies high in the air. But monkeys can look forward when they scramble this way. Kids can't; the best they can do is look down, so they can't tell how far away they are from the platform. They can't even *see* the platform until they've arrived.

Not a good ladder for a mincer like Jack. But when no other kids were nearby screaming, rushing him, or wrestling around under the ladder, he'd sometimes give it a try. I would reach up between the rungs and lightly support Jack's tummy to boost his confidence.

He was three and a half years old the day he stopped in this horizontal section and began to shake.

"You're okay," I told him, while I pushed my hand against his belly more firmly, taking some of the weight off his arms. With the other hand I felt to make sure the bars weren't hot. He continued to shake and began crying out in distress.

Was a bug crawling on him? Had he been stung? Was there something on the rungs that scared him?

Jack was looking down at the sand, which seemed empty. I kicked at it just in case he could see something from his angle that I couldn't see from mine. Nothing.

Now Jack started to scream, and the source of his fear no longer mattered. I pushed him up off the ladder and worked to thread him down between the rungs while he kicked and swatted with fright. The physics from my position made Jack heavier and harder to handle. It was one of those moments when I really needed help. —being an AutiMom can be downright lonely. I nearly dropped him, and he banged every limb against one bar or another as I pulled him through. The moment his feet touched the sand he was running. He scrambled up to the grass and dashed another 15 feet before turning back and issuing a full bend-at-the-waist bellow at the play structure.

What on Earth?!

I pulled my big "park outing" bag and off my shoulder, dropped it into the sand, and climbed up the ladder to investigate. I felt for goo or grease or anything that might have changed the security of Jack's grip. Nothing. Nor was there any left-behind toy or clothing, no trash… There wasn't any wind, no odd smells …

The only sound I heard was Jack, who was now yelling at *me*. He had "fired the play structure" and was ready to leave!

No-Go Zones for Grown Ups

I know you've done it: Climbed up the
playland tube contraption, wiggled into
the netted treehouse over the game room
at Chuck E. Cheese's, and dove head-first
into a stinky ball pit – all to lure, engage
or extract your child. Had trouble getting
back out on occasion? Yep. Been there!
Other parents may stare, but so what? I
consider it proof that your child is more
important to you than theirs are to them.
Boom, girlfriend! Give 'em a little wave.
Any second now their eyes will shift back
to their phones.

Almost directly below me was the shadow of the ladder. It wrinkled as it travelled across the sand, but the rectangle spaces between the rungs were as sharp as the ladder I stood on. Real and shadow ladder-grids overlapped. "Groovy," was the word that popped into my head. Better yet, I could see the shadow of the platform! So even though I couldn't see the platform ahead of me, I could tell from the shadows that it was six rungs away.

I climbed up another step. Shadow Me reached out for the next Shadow Rung. When they met, I shifted my weight forward only to feel Real Hand slip through the bars! I turned my head to protect my face as I slammed against the ladder, shoulder-first. The momentum caused my body to roll, and for a moment thought I was going fall six feet down to the sand on my back!

"#*$%!!"

Yep, I let that one fly. To a nonverbal kid, a curse word is just another word, so that's handy. But right then I was busy worrying what would happen to Jack if I slammed to the ground and severed my spinal cord. I was so ready to join Jack in firing this play structure.

When my balance returned, I scrambled off the ladder, grabbed the park bag and walked over to take my son's hand. The car was way over on the far side of the park. We walked in silence, my heart still hammering.

With the ladder behind us, Jack's mood, however, turned serene. I envied the way he could reset himself. He took the juice box I offered.

Had he been thrown off by the shadow ladder, too? Maybe the sun was brighter than usual today, making the shadow more obvious? Or perhaps the sun was farther north in the sky, casting the shadows straighter down into the climber's line of sight? Maybe Jack noticed the shadow today because he was finally comfortable enough on the ladder to look beyond the bars? I would never know for sure. Bottom line: Jack was done with his favorite play structure. He wouldn't go near it again.

The Guessing Game

Who knows what drives our non-verbal
kids. We weigh the obvious factors, reach
conclusions and tweak those conclusions
again and again as new information comes
in. It's all we can ask of ourselves. But you
know, I think we get it right more than
50% of the time, which literally ain't half
bad. Fist bump, girlfriend.

And that brings me to my main mystery tale. See if you can
figure this one out faster than I did! (Warning: If you do, I'm going
to cry.)

It began the morning I found Jack asleep on the living room couch.
He typically cuckooed in and out of bed all night, but he always
returned to his own bed. This couch business was new. While I
worked on breakfast, he roused and stumbled up the stairs to his
room. He was six at the time; a full six years away from answering a
"why" question.

Of course, the day's avalanche of mini-emergencies soon buried
the incident. I forgot all about it until well after everyone had gone
to bed. I was dipping in and out of sleep myself when I rose to

near wakefulness. … *Did…I hear Jack come down the stairs again? What is he looking for…?* I told myself to go check, but slipped into another dream instead. It may have been a while before I actually got up.

Across the room, I could see the dark curl of Jack's form on the couch. The closer I got, the colder he looked. I lifted him into my arms and paused. Goose bumps transferred from his skin to mine as I stood there thinking. Carrying my four-foot baby up to his room while I was half asleep didn't seem all that wise, but I don't remember making any decision. I just remember standing there.

My alarm went off and I got up. The room was washed in morning light. As I robotically began making the bed, I ran across Jack's binky. Which meant… I must have brought him in here last night. But he wasn't here now.

The peace in our home revolved around that yellow plastic guard with its rubbery tip. The binky was not meant for children with teeth, and Jack shredded his way through one every couple of weeks. MAM, of course, no longer sold this model. *Do manufacturers wait for our kids to glom onto something before gleefully discontinuing it?!* Sure feels that way. A dwindling few online vendors were charging ransom-level prices — $8 a unit, with $4-per-unit shipping — while laughing at that one pathetic woman in the Rockies who kept ordered them.

Jack loved his binky, yet he left it behind to go to his room. So… if his room ranked above even the binky, why was he coming downstairs at night?

I sat down with a cup of coffee trying to Sherlock this through. The unknowns outnumbered the knowns at least 10-to-1. But! There could be more knowns I didn't know were knowns because their link to the unknowns were still unknown. You know? This called for a flow chart!

Getting To Why

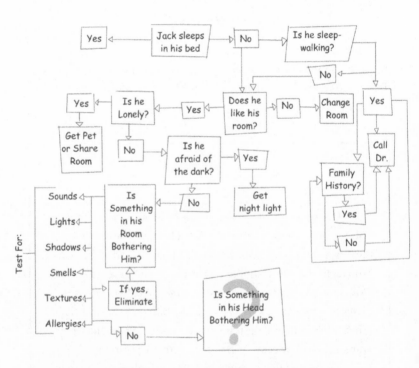

Don't give me that look. You already knew I'm a psycho-mom. Anyway, we're all doing the same thing, even if we don't write it down in boxes: We keep checking through possibilities until something proves right! Or… until they all prove wrong and we're out of ideas, at which point we learn to live with the mystery.

So. My mission today was to vet every possibility listed on this chart and work to eliminate it.

1. **Allergies:** I cleaned his room, checking along the way for anything new:

   - ☑ A stray weed flowering in his potted plant? No.
   - ☑ Pollen on his windowsill? No.
   - ☑ Signs of a mouse in his room? No.
   - ☑ Mold in the vaporizer? Nope.
   - ☑ Dusty vents? I vacuumed them again anyway.

2. **Odors:**

   - ☑ No new scent had been introduced to the room.
   - ☑ I changed his bed sheets, and smelled both mattress and pillows before re-sheeting them.
   - ☑ I smelled the curtains.
   - ☑ I checked behind the book shelf for any snack that may have slipped down and grown moldy.
   - ☑ I cleaned the fish tank.

3. **Textures:**

   - ☑ Jack's pajamas and bedding materials hadn't changed.
   - ☑ Laundry soap was the same since forever.
   - ☑ His favorite blankie was beginning to shred, if that meant anything.
   - ☑ Growing pains? Maybe. I made a note to give him Motrin before bed.

4. **Noise:**

☑ Water flowed continuously over the fish tank filter, and one of Jack's five wall clocks was a ticker. Both sounds were familiar, however, so neither were likely a problem. Here at the back of the house, traffic sounds were almost non-existent. Maybe it was a night-only noise?

☑ Crickets

☑ Owls

☑ Wild animals fighting below his window

☑ And I'm out of ideas.

The options on my chart, however, were starting to thin. I was making progress. From this point on, I would need Jack's input.

Jack was at an age where he could answer yes or no questions, but if he was deeply focused on something else, or was otherwise irritated by my presence, his answers became unreliable.

"Jack, are you a zebra?"

"YES!"

"Jack, am I your mother?"

"NO! Bye-bye!!"

"Jack, do I beat you and lock you in the basement without food for days?"

"YES! YES!"

You can see how this could be problematic.

So that evening, I gave myself 20 extra pre-bedtime minutes in Jack's room. Between questions, I did a little busy work.

"Jack, is there an owl outside your window at night?"

"No."

(Straighten books and CDs.)

"Jack, would you like me to close your curtain?

"No."

(Stack papers, feed fish.)

"Is the fish tank too bright?"

"No."

(Shoes to closet, gather laundry.)

"I can leave the light on in the closet if you like."

"No."

(Empty trash can under desk.)

"Does this shadow on the wall bother you?"

"Ahhh!" He gave me the wrist-wave shoo: No more questions, Mom.

"Sorry." I walked over to pull the covers up and stroke his soft hair. "You are leaving your room to sleep on the couch. Maybe you don't like your room at night? I want to help." Jack looked at me, listening, perhaps understanding, perhaps not, unable to answer regardless. He inserted the gnawed binky into his mouth. I kissed his head. "Good night, my love."

I left the light on in his closet anyway and pulled the door to the sliver-point. I took one last look around the room for anything glaring I might have missed, but the only thing bothering him was apparently me. He removed the binky from his mouth to give me a final, complaining, "Ahhh!"

"Okay. I'm leaving."

The next morning, I was pleased to find Jack was not on the couch.

I tiptoed up to his room.

He wasn't in the bed either.

He was on the floor. He had taken the pillow, his binky and the shredded baby blanket with him, and was curled in a ball to stay warm.

This evidence of attempted self-reliance was enough to break my heart. Either my questions the night before had invaded Jack's privacy as he dealt with whatever this was, or I had given him the impression that coming downstairs was "wrong," and he had adjusted his self-help remedy accordingly. I pulled the bedspread off the bed, gently covered him up, and crept from his room.

Sitting down with a big coffee mug, I reviewed the flow chart. Jack wasn't trying to avoid his room, he was avoiding his bed.

No, we didn't have bed bugs! No more chips for you until you apologize!

Seriously. His bed was exactly the same as it had been since he graduated from the crib. Why was it suddenly threatening?

I traced the chart with my finger until I got to the box with the question mark. Then, like one of those billboards that's been sliced into rotating strips causing the entire billboard image to change as the strips rotate in unison – I'm really overworking this metaphor, but stay with me a moment: first I see a diagram with no logical answer, then the strips rotate and I see a complete answer that was so perfect, I knew immediately it was right! I was exhilarated!

Did you beat me to it?

Jack was having nightmares.

Until our kids are verbal, the world inside their heads may be more powerful than the five senses that link them to reality. This must increase the power of a nightmare more than I care to imagine. We can't cure this problem, but we can help: Weighted blankets, night lights and environmental noise can keep a nonverbal child's mind better-tethered to the outside world.

Take a moment and think of what a nightmare actually is: A custom-developed horror show that plays right inside our heads when we're at our must vulnerable. Most of us begin having them around the age of three, and that first one is mortally terrifying.

You probably still remember yours. When it happens, we need our parents to rescue us! They must come in, turn on the lights, sit beside us and coo repeatedly, "It's okay. It's just a dream," while we drift off again in safety.

Without that parental feedback, Jack had no way of knowing that these horror shows weren't real. He didn't know why they were coming, but he knew where he was when they came. So, he blamed his bed.

Too early for margaritas? Fine, bring me a double-expresso, 'cause *this* was an emergency. I needed a solution that I could put in place for him TODAY. I called his dad, I called my mom, and I called Jack's lead therapist, each time blubbering into the phone so thoroughly that it's a wonder I didn't electrocute myself.

When you finally figure out what your child needs, you can be overwhelmed with guilt. It's horrible. But the only way to avoid that guilt is by never figuring it out.

Social Stories

I'd heard of them, but I'd never seen one actually used. It felt like the right tool for the job, however, especially since these days Jack could decipher written words better than he could grasp spoken ones. And besides, if I had let ignorance stand in my way, I'd never have done anything my whole life. So I jumped right in. This is what it looked like:

Sometimes when I'm asleep
I have bad thoughts
or dreams that scare me.

But they aren't real.
They can't hurt me.
They are only dreams,

and when I wake up,
they go away.

Short easy sentences and simple drawings. I waited until Jack had finished his after-school snack. He was relaxed, and bedtime was still hours away. I brought the story into his room and invited him to sit beside me on the bed.

Jack looked at the paper as I read through it, but he wasn't really listening. (Every day our kids have incomprehensible lessons shoved on them by somebody-or-other, and they get pretty good at pretending to pay attention.) I spoke with animation and pointed to the pictures as I went. His eyes calmly followed my fingers to the end of the text.

Then his face changed and my heart leaped. It was working!

He leaned in, really looking at the story. I read it again, watching as he bore down into the information. He put a hand on the story and looked up at me.

"Here," I told him. "Your turn."

Jack took the page in both hands and began reading the story aloud with "Mom's animation." He paused in the same places I had paused to point out the same pictures. With each pause, he looked at me with a huge, "stimmy" smile. When he finished the story, he jumped off the bed and began pacing the room, looking at the story and pacing again. The air grew so thick with his relief that it was like the room had filled with Jello. He squealed and flapped in a circle, then took two steps to his desk where he placed the story by his keyboard. Arms back, fingers twitching, Jack look down on the story and read it again.

I'm still not sure if this is what a social story should look like, but it was just what my son needed: I'd never seen Jack so happy. My job was done. Before leaving his room, I stepped behind Jack and kissed the top of his head. He didn't even notice.

33

Coming Soon!

Holy cow. You know that friend who has the most angelic little three-year-old who sits at the table with the adults, listening calmly, never fussing? Then that same friend has a second child, and the three year old turns into the Tasmanian Devil? Sheesh! *We* thought *our* kiddos were handfuls! Am I right? Ha-ha-ha-ha! Snort!

Wooo! Ha-ha-ha! Ahem.

Uh-oh…

What's going to happen to *our* kids when a younger sibling arrives?! That's a… well, it's… kind of a… scary… thought.

Yeah.

Because, look at the scenario that plays out in a neurotypical home: Kid B comes along and suddenly Kid A loses a big slab of parental attention. Kid B cries unless he's sleeping, then everyone has to whisper and sneak around the house, which is boring. Kid A won't be able to play with Kid B until he's, like, a million years older. Meanwhile, Kid B, horror of horrors, might get moved right into Kid A's room, complete with nap schedule and dirty diaper pail!! The resentment makes total sense.

But I think there's something more primal in the mix that could be especially hard for spectrum kids to grapple with: Breach of faith. An unspoken trust between the Parents and Kid A is broken with the arrival of Kid B. Here's what I mean:

Imagine that you married the perfect guy and you're living this wonderful, harmonious life, with mice mending your clothes and bluebirds trimming your pie crusts. Then one day, hubby brings home a second bride. He compliments her endlessly, rushes to her side every time she sighs, and he gives her half of your closet space. Later, while she's wined and dined at the table you bought *before you even met this man,* you're left in the kitchen loading the dishwasher.

"Resentment" no longer covers it.

Within 24 hours, you'd be gone; Notice of Intent from divorce lawyer to follow, right? But Kid A doesn't have that option. All he can do is scream about it. And bite Kid B on the shoulder. Yep, he's probably doing that when Mom's not looking.

An entire Advice Industry has erected itself around preparing Kid A for the sibling-to-come. Fortunately, those thousands of blogs and articles can be distilled into a single paragraph, which — since I want you reading *my* stuff and not *theirs* — I am pleased to supply below. It helps to mentally play some new-agey music as you read it:

Talk to your child. Bring the new baby into the family months ahead of time through conversation. Let your child ask questions. Show your child her own baby photos. Tell her how she behaved as a newborn and explain how the new baby will be similar.

— End Music

Well isn't that jolly.

Our kids don't understand us when we call them to dinner! How the heck are we going to converse with them about something they've never experienced and which won't be happening for months?! Honestly, I don't know why we google this crap when we know, for us, it's going to be nothing but shredder fodder. It's a waste of time and energy, and it leaves us feeling bad about our families, *but we keep doing it.* Yes, of <u>course</u> I'm guilty too. We're all hoping to find something brilliant that can be modified for our situation, but I'm telling you, girlfriend, it's a trap.

Modify, Schmodify

Some of the advice columns and blogs out there are really good, and it's tempting to want to take that advice and modify it. Like... instead of telling your kid a new baby is coming, take your kid to see your next sonogram! What a great idea...

(Not)!

Now your nonverbal and utterly traumatized child thinks an alien is growing inside of you and that it's only a matter of time before he gets one too! Try fixing *that* without words to help you!

When we modify good advice, it somehow magically turns into a steaming pile. Give up already. What we really need to do is construct our own good advice from scratch. We can do this by asking ourselves, in the tiniest, most basic terms, what it is we hope to accomplish.

In the case of a younger sibling, the goal is to prepare our kids for the new life that will soon be entering the home. So we need to think carefully about what that really mean to our kids:

- ☑ Sharing parent time
- ☑ Learning to be gentle
- ☑ Developing patience
- ☑ Tolerating new noises
- ☑ Giving up some space
- ☑ Acclimating to new smells — often unpleasant ones
- ☑ Helping care for the needs of another being
- ☑ Finding enjoyment in this new creature

These are all learnable skills. Our goal, now, is to help Kid A get started on these skills before Kid B arrives. Here's how that translated into a plan for Jack. Your child, of course, is different, but some of this plan may be worth borrowing.

Tray Tables Up, Prepare For Arrival

Jack was three when I was pregnant with his sister. Everyone pretty much agrees that three is *the worst age* for a child to be when a new sibling joins the family. (Sigh) Of course it is. We were on a non-stop flight to double hockey sticks and would soon arrive at our destination if I didn't figure something out.

In my second trimester, I bought a bird cage, seed, nest and two noisy finches. I got it all set up in the store, allowing me to just walk through the front door with them, fait accompli. Ta-da! They flapped about with great commotion, and when Jack walked over, they all but cursed at him. Startled, he backed away from the cage and looked at me.

"Birds," I said with a happy smile.

For the first few days, I carried the cage with me from room to room. Jack watched as I fed the finches, talked to them, changed the paper at the bottom of the cage, and draped the cage at night with towels. I didn't cheat Jack out of any time with me, but sometimes I tended the birds first.

Heh? Do you see what I'm doing here?

Jack circled the birds for a few days, curious but wary. By Day Three, he found himself laughing at the clumsy way they hopped about. On Day Four, he was ready to interact. His chosen path: Smacking the side of the cage to make them squawk and fly into each other.

This is exactly what I did not want him
doing to his baby sister. It's also why I
chose animals that were protected inside
a cage.

"They're funny, huh," I said with a big smile as I sat down on
the other side of the cage. I put my hand on top of his. "Let's be
gentle. They're little and we're big. Let's be gentle."

I had a small mound of dryer lint handy. I poked a few pieces
through the bars of the cage and the birds quickly grabbed them
and took them into the nest. "Gentle," I repeated. I handed Jack a
pinch of lint. He pushed it through the bars and let it drop to the
cage floor.

The male finch popped out of the nest, hopped down for the
lint and flapped back up to the nest. The female took the lint from
the male's beak and pressed it into the nest, adjusting it, adjusting
it, and readjusting it again. She was so clearly "making the bed,"
that it was almost cartoony. Jack laughed and reached out for
another piece of lint. I passed him one pinch at a time, and we
spent the next 15 minutes watching the birds put their nest
together.

The birds became familiar and accepted. Their noise no longer
distracted Jack. He liked hanging out with them while he watched
videos. He learned to wedge triangles of bread between the bars of
the cage for them to peck at. He even helped me put the towels on
the cage at night.

Stage one was complete.

In my 3rd trimester, I brought home a bigger cage. This one had
a very active mouse in it that climbed up and down three levels of
ladders. The bottom level also had a wire wheel that he would dash
in so aggressively that when he stopped, the wheel would continue
turning, taking the mouse around with it in a full, backwards circle.
Another weird thing: It would clamor up to the third level, grab the
roof of the cage with its front feet and then dangle itself for five
seconds or so before letting go and dropping three levels straight
down to the bottom of the cage. It would then clamor back up and
do it again.

Jack loved this mouse from Day One, even though it was
hugely stinky; even though it jerked and scrambled about
unpredictably; even though it caused nonstop thumping, rattling
and squeaking noise.

(Confession: I wasn't that fond of the mouse.)

After maybe a week, I got one of those plastic run-about balls.
The mouse took to it like an Indy 500 driver at a demolition derby.

It would streak across the room, then
crash into every single leg of a chair
before reaching another clear stretch of
floor where it would streak again. Jack
would squeal and run after it. Mickey was
the best "toy" in the world.

Over the next few days, I taught Jack
not to kick the ball while the mouse was
in it. I taught him that a mouse-filled ball
should not be thrown, spun, or placed at the top of the staircase.
Each lesson unfortunately came after I realized it was needed (sorry
Mickey). "Let's be gentle," I told Jack. "The mouse is little and

we're big. Let's be gentle."

So, now Jack had a living creature that moved around the house at will; a creature who would bring his stink with him, invited or not. Jack had to watch what he was doing and where he was stepping, remaining alert to the whereabouts of this other being. He needed to be careful and gentle with this creature, even as he enjoyed it.

Heh? Heh? Is this smart or what!

Another couple of weeks had passed when the finch nest was suddenly filled with hatchlings. This was an unintentional Plan Bonus – honestly, I didn't know caged birds would do this without a breeder to help them! But one morning, I took off the towels and there they were. Their tiny chorus of peeps was magical.

"Look, Jack!" I called him over to watch the parents feed their hatchlings. "Look! Babies! Babies in the nest! The birds had babies!" What a perfect moment to push this new word. I spoke it clearly, slowly, and with lively animation. Jack watched the nest activity without smiles or flaps, just the blank face of a boy performing broadband data-uptake.

Okay… This observation was not going onto his mental "Disney Shelf."

I took a fresh look at the hatchlings: They were naked, bulgy and spindly. Blue-black lids covered their eyes. They looked more small potato bugs, than birds – i.e. not charming *at all*. Jack may have been wondering how five bulb-headed, fleshy insects had gotten into the nest, and if the parent birds were feeding them or trying to eat them. Suddenly unsure if I wanted the word "baby" attached to this scene, I cut the lesson short.

As my due date drew closer, the hatchlings took on the look of real birds. They grew fat and feathery, and their faces crowded together at the entrance to the nest. Although Mickey was still his favorite, Jack now found the hatchlings interesting. Over a matter of days, one by one they each cartwheeled out of the nest to sit along the perch and peep noisily at the larger world.

That's when it occurred to me: This cage was meant for two birds. Now there were seven! The perch was wall-to-wall with their bodies. They jostled and pecked at each other. They flapped and pooped on each other. But what could I do? I couldn't give any of them away right now. Can you imagine? What would *that* lesson be?

1. Mom and Dad have babies

2. Mom and Dad feed babies

3. Babies are taken by strangers

So, no. The birds were staying.

Meanwhile, the overall plan was working well: First we got birds, then a mouse, then five hatchlings, and finally… a baby sister.

I was gone a few days while I "acquired this final pet."

Upon returning home, I set the baby carrier aside while I received Jack's hug and annoyed him with a smothering of kisses. He ran off to chase the mouse without glancing once at the carrier. I settled into the sofa with the baby and waited for Jack to notice his sister in his own time. It took about ten minutes.

Jack stopped running and stared. He gnawed thoughtfully on his binky a moment before walking over. He looked down on his sister's sleeping face. He started to touch her, then changed his mind. She wasn't that interesting, but at least she didn't look like a potato bug.

I took the tiny binky out her mouth. I then took Jack's binky and held them up side by side. They were the same color and shape, only Jack's was twice the size. "Jack," I said, holding up the bigger model. I held up the smaller, saying, "Baby."

I pretended to put the bigger one into his sister's mouth by mistake, which made him laugh. He grabbed his binky and stood there chewing on it, considering this new pet. Then the mouse rattled past in the ball. Sorry; mouse beats sister. He ran off after it.

Few things are more sleep-inducing than holding a sleeping baby. I stretched out on the sofa and closed my eyes. I probably did nod off for a bit – enough not to notice that Jack had returned. When his hand brushed my arm, I opened my eyes to find him petting his sister on the head.

"Baby," he said. Then he turned and ran after the mouse again.

34

Between Friends

We're getting close to the end here, so it's time for some straight talk. There are days when every AutiMom is downright pissed.

Why can't our kids be the ones doing handspring-back-flips in gymnastics class, or winning all the swim meet medals, or even joining a soccer league?

Why can't they be the ones mastering Chinese and French?

Why do we have to spend 45 minutes preparing our child for a 30 minute trip to the grocery store – a trip that all too often ends with us abandoning our carts to tow a screaming child back to the car while shoppers rubberneck, clerks frown, and the occasional pencil-browed gum-smacker "captures the moment on video" thinking this upload might earn her a million subscribers and a booking on Jimmy Kimmel?

Why, when our parental workload is three-times greater than other mothers, are we the ones people shake their heads at? Why are we approached by strangers with pointed advice? Why is *our* child the only one stepping off the school bus without a party invitation in hand? Sometimes we just want to slug someone! Not our kids, of course, but almost anyone else within swinging distance.

Other days we just want to cry. We all get tired of being this tired, and we know that no matter how hard we push, for many of us "normal life" is never going to return. We know we'll never ask our 14 year old to get the spaghetti started or to mow the lawn. We know our 16 year old will never run errands for us in exchange for borrowing the car. Our 18 year old will not head off for college, and our 27 year old will not get married, move away and buy a home of his own.

Even many of us with higher-functioning kids fear that the laundry, meal prep, chauffeuring, house cleaning and personal care work will go on and on; that there will be no parental cutoff-point anywhere on the horizon. And for those among us who have seen partners jump ship, the likelihood of finding a new partner who will accept both us and our child as a lifelong set seems impossible.

Then, while our siblings and friends plan exotic trips and have money left over for their retirements, we forgo both as "luxuries" and instead frantically cram a few dollars at a time into a disability trust; a trust that may need to support our kids for 50 years after we're gone. Of course we want to cry. I often do myself, so go ahead; you'll feel better afterwards. I'll wait.

Fair warning, though: I'm eating the chips.

The thing is, none of us are sure where this journey is headed. We're all just hanging on, hoping for the best. And as scary as it seems at times, you are not alone. You are among friends — there are so many of us. We are an enormous club of AutiMoms, and we understand you in a way your family and friends no longer can. We will always be rooting for you, laughing with you, weeping with you, fist-pumping your every success, and groaning with your every gripe.

And let me tell you something: I am not a particularly religious person, but I'm confident God did not give you your child as some kind of punishment. Oops, did I actually write that? Yes! You'd be surprised how many AutiMoms have felt that way at one time or other. Don't you dare blame yourself! A don't let anyone guilt you into it, be they parent or PhD-wielding guest lecturer.

That said, I believe all things unfold as they do for a reason. I think society may need your child for a purpose we can't yet see. And I believe God rewarded your child *with the gift of you*. He saw you as smarter, more intuitive, more determined, more flexible and simply more capable of raising this beautiful child to the full potential required of him. Your child needed *you*, he deserved *you*, so God placed him on your doorstep.

Girlfriend, you're doing a magnificent job.

ABOUT THE AUTHOR

Prior to becoming an AutiMom, Jack's Mom spent 10 years in the film, advertising and fashion industries of Europe and Asia, working as a writer, project manager and choreographer. She then spent another decade launching and running a visitor center design and development firm. By the time her children were born, she was well versed in multiple languages and cultures, and was a respected "experiential show" developer. This fruitful and established life came to an end the day her son was diagnosed. Every skill she ever developed was now critical to her as she raised a child with autism.

Today Jack's Mom is a member of the Board of Directors of the Arc of the Pikes Peak Region, on behalf of whom she often speaks to reporters and live audiences. She is also a regular contributor to the Arc's Autism Blog.

Made in the USA
Coppell, TX
24 July 2021